Where the Yellow Arrows Lead

Adam Bailey

For Julie, my fellow pilgrim on life's journey.

Chapters

Foreword

Let me first say that this is less of a foreword and more of disclaimer. I am not a writer. I am a high school Spanish teacher; so, while you may learn a word or two in Spanish, if you don't already know the language, do not expect this to be some great work of literature. In fact, do not expect much of anything, as I am not entirely sure myself what this book is meant to be. It started as a travel journal, but grew into something more. It is a memoir, certainly, but I venture into essays on spirituality, religion and my experience with Catholicism. You will find poetry, but it is not an anthology of any kind. If you picked this up thinking it was a guide to walking the Camino, you will not find it very practical. The chapters do not follow a chronological or geographical order necessarily. They are more reflections on thoughts I had along the way. At its core, I guess, it is a love story.

Where the Yellow Arrows Lead is a story of how I went on a journey along an ancient pilgrimage road on my way to get married. The road was marked by yellow arrows, but I realized that many other arrows were pointing me in the direction of love even before I started walking. So, who should read this? Who is the intended audience? I guess it is for my kids if one day they might ask why I married their mother. It is for Julie, as a testament of my love for her, and a sort of renewal of my vows that I made in the Chapel of Santa María "La Antigua" Corticela on our wedding day. It is for anyone who has thought about making a pilgrimage or has wondered if people find God or encountered miracles along the Camino de Santiago.

The Fork

Two roads diverged in a wood, and I...I took.... I took another look at the map hanging around my neck because I didn't remember seeing a fork in the road the last time I checked. This was not Robert Frost's poetic yellow wood of New England. No, the fork in the road I found before me was on the other side of the ocean in Northern Spain. And no matter which road I chose, neither could be considered "less traveled."

You see, I was walking along the pilgrimage route known as the Camino de Santiago, or the Way of St. James, and because millions of people have traveled this road since the Middle Ages, whichever path I chose was going to be pretty well worn. And unlike the Frost poem, where choosing one road rather than the other made all the difference, the choice in front of me at this moment and in this place was relatively inconsequential. I knew where I was going. My destination was planned months ago, and I knew when I had to get there, so choosing which way to go at this fork in the road was not going to be some life-changing decision. I had already come to the life-changing crossroads in my life some seven months earlier when I asked Julie to marry me.

In fact, it was precisely that reason...to get married...that I found myself at this fork in the road along the Camino. You could say I was walking five hundred miles down the aisle to the altar, because that is roughly the distance from the Pyrenees to the city of Santiago de Compostela, where we had arranged to have the wedding. The plan was for me to begin walking on my own from the town of Roncesvalles in the foothills of the Pyrenees and then meet up with Julie when she could come join me. My school year finished earlier, so I had decided to start off on my own. She would then join me on the Camino somewhere between Burgos and Leon, where we would continue walking together until we reached the cathedral in Santiago. It was kind of a metaphor, walking alone was my life as a bachelor, and then walking with Julie, well...we were getting married.

I could have waited to start in order to walk the whole route together, but the chapel of La Corticela was reserved for eight o'clock in the evening of July 8, 2004, so we had a set amount of time to walk it, and if I hoped to walk the entire route, I had to get started. All we needed to do was arrive with enough time to get cleaned up from the weeks of walking, find a dress for Julie, a suit for me, and a couple of wedding rings. At least that was the plan. But now I found myself at a fork in the road that I could not find anywhere on my map with an ocean separating me from the woman I fell in love with and was to marry and most of my five-hundred-mile journey still in front of me

The map I had hanging in a clear plastic pocket holder around my neck was given to me by my friend Antonio, who, being a native of Galicia and a teacher of philosophy and religion, had walked the Camino several times already. He said it would be good to have so that I wouldn't need to continually unpack my backpack and dig out a guidebook every time I wasn't sure where I was. Up until now it was pretty easy to know in which direction to walk, as the path was marked by yellow arrows painted on the rocks, the trees, on the back of street signs, on the side of buildings, on a curb. Pretty much any time I needed to orient myself I could simply look around and spot a painted yellow arrow somewhere. Much of the walk thus far was a single mountain trail leading down from the Pyrenees through woods and pastures and small villages.

The yellow arrows that were painted on rocks or trees or a fence post by a pasture also appeared on sidewalks, cobblestones, or the wall of the corner house as I entered a town along The Camino. The way was pretty obvious most of the time. Walking through the city of Pamplona was a bit more of a challenge, as there were so many more markings that made the yellow arrows harder to spot. Street signs, billboards, flyers stapled to telephone poles, not to mention spray-painted markings on the roads and sidewalks made by municipal utility companies indicating an upcoming construction project...and just the garden variety graffiti, made identifying the yellow arrows I was seeking a bit more like finding Waldo.

And when I did find the yellow arrow camouflaged amidst the city distractions, something in the back of my head was suspicious that it might have been put there by some prankster, just looking to get a laugh at a bunch of naive pilgrims with their silly wooden staffs, funny hats and backpacks trekking off in the wrong direction down some dead-end alley or onto a street under repair.

I don't know why I wasn't suspicious of the painted arrows in the countryside, but I wasn't. It is not as if I had grown up in the countryside and therefore more trusting of being in nature. In fact, the opposite is true. I called Philadelphia my home at the time, as I had been living there almost eight years, and before that I had lived in Washington, D.C. for almost ten. I grew up about a half hour outside of New York City in a New Jersey suburb, so I really was much more accustomed to city life. Yet for some reason, along the

Camino, it was the countryside that made me feel more at ease.

So, when I reached this first big city along my route, I walked quickly through it, only stopping once at a pharmacy to stock up on Ibuprofen and adhesive blister pads. I made it to a hostel on the outskirts of town where I spent the night. The next morning, I would find myself back in the countryside, but it was there, after a couple hours of walking, where I was confounded by a fork in the road that was not showing anywhere on my map.

I turned to Toshi, a Japanese pilgrim I was walking with that morning, and had been walking with the last couple of days, and asked him which way he thought we should go. Toshi was a guy about my age, the best I could tell, with a kind smile that turned down at the edges, jet black hair that escaped from under his waterproof bucket hat as if begging for a haircut that was two weeks overdue. I am guessing he picked up the hat at some souvenir shop on a trip to Singapore as it had "Singapore" in white lettering across the front and tiny paw prints running around the brim. He wore small wire-framed spectacles, a blue fanny pack, and a map in a plastic holder hung around his neck just like mine. He carried a curved tree branch that he most likely found along the path somewhere, but it was a poor excuse for a walking stick. I am pretty certain it would have snapped in two if he had put much weight on it. I am not sure exactly why he picked it up. Maybe he saw other pilgrims with walking sticks and decided he should have one too. Toshi's dark eyes looked at me thoughtfully through his spectacles as he pondered my question about which way to go.

As if stating the obvious, he suggested that I look at the map I had hanging around my neck. At least that is what I think he suggested. I discovered early on in our walking together that Toshi did not speak English or Spanish, and since the only Japanese I knew was *"konichiwa,"* most of our conversation these past couple of days was guessing, based on facial expressions, hand gestures and common experience along the road together. I am pretty sure that he started the Camino a day or two before I did and was walking with his father, but when his father's ankle gave out, he decided to continue on his own with his father's blessing. But then again, with my limited-one-word-vocabulary of Japanese, he could have just met the older Japanese gentleman here in Spain, stolen his wallet while he put down his pack to remove his hiking boots to tend to some blisters, and then took off quickly to avoid being caught. But Toshi seemed like a nice guy, so that is why I surmised the first scenario.

He would smile and nod, as I would talk for a bit while walking, pretending to follow what I was saying, and then I would return the favor of nods and smiles while he chatted about whatever it was that he was talking about. It helped pass the time as we walked and kept me from thinking about my sore feet and aching knees. Anyway, it was either my improving understanding of Japanese, or his pointing with his finger to the map around my neck, that I understood his suggestion. But as I looked again at the map, I still could not find any fork in the road where I estimated our location to be. I let the map hang back down and turned to Toshi and shrugged my shoulders with my arms bent at my sides and palms facing upward, which is the international sign for "I have no clue what to do."

We both looked around again for some suggestive yellow paint, but found none. The road we had just come up was a rural road passing through a pasture with some cows grazing off in the distance, and it now split into a rocky gravel road heading towards the right, into the woods, and a dirt road heading left leading to what looked like a highway in the distance. There were no other pilgrims along this stretch of the Camino that we could see, so nobody to follow. We certainly did not want to walk back to the hostel where we started. A pilgrim on foot learns quickly to economize steps. If you are going to have the stamina to walk fifteen to twenty miles a day or more, you can't afford to do much retracing of steps. We had already walked about five miles that morning, and it was a ways just to get back to the last building we passed, so going back was not an option. I was going to pick one of these roads and go forward. I just wished I knew which way to go.

"*A la derecha hay una fuente y mucha cuesta,*" said a low gravelly voice as if in the back of my head. Toshi heard the voice, too, as we both turned around to see standing behind us a short, ruddy old fellow in a jacket and black boina, a traditional hat worn by the men in this region. He had a weathered face and kind dark eyes, and his dress would suggest he was a local, but where did he come from? We did not pass him on the road. At least I don't think we did.

To be honest, I had not paid much attention to the locals I passed along the Camino. I had stopped the day before to take a picture of this elderly couple working in a field right next to the road I was walking along. The man was holding the handles of an old wooden plow being pulled by a mule. He wore faded blue coveralls that made him look more like a mechanic than a farmer and his snow-white hair separated the blue from his collar from the blue on his baseball cap. An older woman, who I could only assume was his wife, stood behind him in a brown, burlap skirt, wearing boots with white socks pulled up to the knees, a flannel shirt and a green head scarf. She was observing his plowing while holding a hoe in her hand. I imagined the kinds of conversations these two had as they worked the fields together. You knew the fields were plowed by hand as the rows undulated up and down, as if the man were fighting the mule to keep a straight line, but they were evenly spaced, and the soil looked rich and the crops were green. Was she standing behind him telling him to keep the plow straight thinking he was at fault and not the mule? Was she looking on worried that he was too old for this kind of work?

I took the picture because it seemed like a scene out of the past. Spain is a modern industrialized country. Madrid has a sleek, clean subway system that connects the airport to the city center. You can find a Starbuck's and a McDonalds without much effort. But along the Camino de Santiago you can also find a Spain that seems to have been forgotten by time. I didn't stop to talk to the couple. What would I say? I just snapped a picture and moved on. But when Toshi and I found ourselves lost at this fork in the road, it was a local man in a black boina who stopped to talk to us, two foreign travelers clearly in need of some direction.

"*A la izquierda, cuatro fuentes y más llano*," he said pointing to the left. As if in answer to our dilemma, he told us the path to the right would have a fountain, but would be hilly, while the road to the left provided four fountains along a more flat countryside. Toshi and I turned back to look at our options. The right path looked the more inviting, with pine trees shading the walk and what promised to be a more picturesque landscape. But looking to the left, I thought of the benefit of being able to fill my canteen more often so that I would not have to be so stingy taking sips to keep me hydrated as I walked. My knees were also pleading with me to opt for the less hilly route, as the downhill treks were starting to become painful.

I wondered what Toshi was thinking. We looked at each other, both with a look of decision on our faces, and as we turned back to thank the old man who had given us the information we needed to make up our minds, he was gone. We looked around but could not see him anywhere. Were we standing their pondering our route longer than we realized and, in that time, had he walked back down the road or into the pasture to tend to the cows? Did he go behind a tree to attend to nature's call? He went just as mysteriously as he came. Whatever the explanation, we were happy for his help and headed off down the road to the left.

I never had the chance to thank this man. I never learned his name. I never asked him how he knew we needed some guidance as we stopped at that fork in the road. He had answered our question without it ever being asked out loud. He was like a guardian angel sent to make sure we continued on the right path. And as soon as he completed his mission, poof, he was gone. Toshi and I didn't talk about him. We just continued our walk until we spotted the next yellow arrow, letting us know we were still on the right road. We walked together for the rest of that day.

The local man in the black boina was correct about the fountains. There was one fountain, however, that was unlike any other we had come across on the Camino. It was the fountain at the Bodegas Irache, a winery just outside the town of Estella. That particular fountain had separate spigots offering two very different choices: water or red wine! Toshi and I turned to each other and grinned as if we had just discovered the most marvelous attraction in all of Spain. We took turns taking pictures of each other drinking from the wine spigot to prove to those back home that this miraculous fountain truly existed. I imagined the old boina-wearing Spaniard smiling and giving us a wink, as if to say we chose our path wisely.

If life should ever present you with an unexpected fork in the road, imagine talking about your options with someone who doesn't speak your language. If the answer doesn't come to you, be prepared for the unexpected local who knows the lay of the land to give you some advice. Realize that turning back is not an option, and what lays ahead may hold some welcomed surprises you did not anticipate. I know I am starting with a story that does not coincide with the beginning of my pilgrimage, but a fork in the road is a place where we must make choices, and those choices are like new beginnings. So, when does a journey begin, really? Allow me to retrace my steps and go back to where I started walking the Camino.

The Riddle

"When you are walking the Camino, is it better to look down, keeping your eyes on the ground so that you avoid tripping over a tree root, twisting an ankle on a rock or stepping in mud? Or is it better to keep your head up, looking forward and around you to keep your bearings, to see the path ahead, and to appreciate the sights and beauty that surround you?"

This was the question that my friend Antonio posed to me as I was on the eve of my first day walking the Camino. He was not going to walk with me, but he had picked me up from the airport in Madrid and drove me to Roncesvalles, where I was to start my pilgrimage. He was in many ways my guide for this journey. He was the one to pick up a guidebook, a map, a lightweight blue aluminum canteen, a Nokia cell phone, and my scallop shell.

The scallop shell is something that pilgrims walking the Camino de Santiago will wear to let others know that they are on official pilgrimage. It is a tradition that started centuries ago when pilgrims would walk to Santiago, continue to the coast of Galicia, and pick up a scallop shell that was commonly found along the beaches to prove they had reached their destination.

Nowadays the white shells, painted with the cross of the order of St. James, can be found in many souvenir shops along the Camino, and are still worn by those making the walk. I also heard that it is customary for someone to present you with a shell as you set out...good luck or something.

Antonio had also obtained *La Credencial del Peregrino*, the official pilgrim's passport, which was used to show at the hostels, *refugios* or albergues as they are called in Spanish, so that you could get lodging overnight, many of which did not charge, but would accept donations. "Pilgrim, leave what you can, take what you need," said a handwritten sign at the entrance to one of the *refugios*.

While probably not the best business model if you were trying to make a living in the hospitality industry today, it did embody the spirit of hospitality along the Camino. The word "hospitality" comes from the Latin hospes, meaning a stranger or foreigner, and hospitium, signifying the relation between a stranger and one who provides shelter. A fellow teacher, and Latinist, always refers to this word with her students as a two-way street of mutual trust and friendliness. Dating back to the Middle Ages, people would provide shelter and aid to foreigners who were on pilgrimage to Santiago, giving them a place to sleep, a meal, and often tend to their ailments and injuries sustained along the road. So not only is the word "hospitality" linked to the Camino, but so are "hotel," and "hospital."

Nowadays it is very hard to imagine either a hotel or a hospital with a sign at the entrance saying you can take what you need and leave what you can, but it is nice to think that there was such a time, and that the spirit lives on along this road to Santiago. In any case, Antonio brought me to the first pilgrim's hostel in Roncesvalles where I got the folded document with designated spaces for the hospitalero to place a stamp indicating you passed that way.

You see the purpose of *La Credencial del Peregrino* was twofold. You needed it to prove you were a registered pilgrim to gain access to the hostels, and each time you entered a hostel and got your stamp, your pilgrim's passport would fill up to prove that you did indeed complete the pilgrimage. Not that you need to prove anything to anyone, as this journey is a profoundly personal one, as this tale will soon tell, but if you present your credentials to the pilgrim's office next to the cathedral in Santiago de Compostela, you will receive an official Compostellana, a document written in Latin declaring you an "official pilgrim." You do need to walk at least one hundred kilometers to get one. My plan was to walk about seven hundred and fifty kilometers by starting in Roncesvalles. I expected it would take me a little less than a month to complete, but I had a deadline to meet. I needed to arrive in Santiago on a particular day.

Now I would not recommend having a firm deadline for completing the pilgrimage, as it is not easy to know ahead of time how fast you could walk, or if injury will slow you down. There are many pilgrims, some of whom I met along the way, who only walk part of the Camino. Some have limited time off from work and only choose to walk certain stages of the path. Others will not be able to continue due to injury or exhaustion and will cut short their journey, as in the case of Toshi's father, or Mary and Geraldine, two Irish septuagenarians I met on the road into Pamplona and then again in Navarette. And there are some that will simply become disillusioned with the experience and not see the point of continuing. But in my case, I had no choice. I had to be at the Cathedral of Santiago by eight in the evening on July eighth. That's when I was getting married.

It was my wedding I was thinking about when I responded, "for religious reasons," when the hospitalera, who gave me my pilgrim's passport and registered me there in Roncesvalles, asked me why I was walking the Camino de Santiago. She would ask each pilgrim as they requested a *credencial* for their purpose for walking. Apparently, this information was part of the registration process. You could choose one of three options: religious, spiritual, or cultural.

Truth be told, I could have picked any one of those options, but as I looked at the expression on the hospitalera's face, the same stern expression of inquisition my fourth-grade teacher Mrs. Moulton would give when she would turn around from the blackboard hearing some noise and want a confession about what mischief was going on, I knew I wanted to keep my response simple and defensible. My purpose was religious. If she pressed me for more information, I would tell her it was because I was getting married by a Catholic priest in a rite of holy matrimony at the end of my walk. That would be enough to explain it. She looked at me with a raised eyebrow, but did not ask me for any further explanation.

With my stamped credencial in hand, I had everything I needed to take my first steps as a pilgrim. This brings me back to Antonio's question as I was about to head out. Is it better to walk with your head up or walk with your head down? I should have known that the answer would be embedded with some sage advice that provoked a more profound consideration of the question, and I didn't anticipate the false dilemma. "The answer," he said, "is that it is better to walk with a friend."

While the irony of his answer was not lost on me, as he was not going to accompany me on my journey, the point he was making was that we should learn to rely on others to help us through our journey of life. Too often we Americans glorify the Lone Ranger hero who goes it alone. I don't know if there is some gratification in being able to take all the credit for successes along the way if nobody has pitched in to help, or if there is some fear that asking for help is a sign of weakness, but I must admit that I feel this cultural impulse to want to "do it by myself." I know there are other cultures that place importance on the group and that taking credit for individual achievement is actually frowned upon, but I did not grow up in such a culture. And while I knew that Julie would be joining me soon enough along the Camino, I admit I was excited by the challenge of walking alone for the first couple of weeks. But I had not even taken my first step along the road to Santiago when I learned the lesson Antonio was trying to teach me.

Antonio had left to return to Madrid after making sure I had everything I needed for the trek and wishing me a *"Buen Camino."* I found a café near the first hostel I would stay at in Roncesvalles, sat down at a table by myself to have dinner, and contemplated the journey before me. The restaurant experience in Spain is very different than in America. The waiters do not constantly attend to you, or ask how everything is, or try to engage in friendly banter in hopes of earning a more generous tip. In fact, waiters in Spain can appear to the American customer as standoffish, negligent or even rude. But when you recognize the cultural context of the restaurant scene, where the waiter does not consider himself to be part of your eating experience, but rather is there to simply bring you what you need and allow you to enjoy the food and the time sitting at your own pace.

You did not come to the restaurant with the hopes of making a new friend with a member of the wait staff. You came to spend quality time with your family or friends and enjoy the food and drink. The Spanish waiter is not working for tips, so if you spend the whole evening sipping coffee and talking with friends, or if you eat a three-course meal in five minutes, there is no difference to the waiter. Unlike in the U.S. where the waiter wants to turn over tables quickly so that there is an opportunity to earn numerous tips from one table at his station throughout the night, the Spanish waiter is happy to stand in the shadows until you request his presence to bring something you need. Hence, what may seem like prompt service and friendliness from an American waiter could be interpreted as a ploy to get you fed and on your way as quickly as possible. You will never hear a Spanish waiter ask, "Are you ready for the check?"

I spent a leisurely evening at the café with a glass of wine, eating tapas and writing in my journal. After I paid the bill, and left a bit more than the required change for a tip due to my ingrained American sense of duty to leave at least fifteen percent, I got my things and headed down the street towards the refugio. Minutes later I heard someone yelling after me running down the street in my direction. It was my waiter waving something in his hand. My first thought was one of horror, "Did I forget to leave a tip?"

I soon realized he was holding my pilgrim's passport, my *credencial* that I would need for the rest of my journey. I had left it at the table. He could easily have cleared the table and thrown away this piece of paper that had no meaning to him, but he didn't. He made the effort to catch me and return the document, knowing that it would be important to me. In terms of Antonio's riddle, I was focusing on the horizon and not on the ground in front of me. I never got the waiter's name, but I thanked him for his kindness. He played the role of the friend on this part of the journey, these first few steps, to help me avoid stumbling.

I must admit, despite the gratitude I felt, I also felt stupid and embarrassed for being such a scatterbrain. What would have happened if he had not found my passport and returned it to me? I would have had to get another one, and perhaps not until the next day if the office were closed, and then I would have to pay for lodging, and I did not even know if there was another place to stay in that town, and all the "what ifs" started running through my head, compounding my sense of shame in my lack of responsibility. I began recounting other moments in my life where I did stupid things because I wasn't paying attention.

Once when I was seven years old, I was standing on a dock on a lake in Maine waiting for my turn to go for a canoe ride with my father. He was paddling around the lake with my sister while I waited standing on the dock with my life jacket on and my paddle in hand. I was alone on the dock. Some of my aunts and uncles were sitting up in the screened-in porch overlooking the lake chatting while playing cribbage. My attention turned towards the life under the surface of the crystal-clear water of Round Pond. If you look at the water at an early hour before the sun is high enough to cause a reflection or early evening when the sun is low, you can see right to the bottom and make out every stone, plant and fish swimming by. I knew there were bass in this particular lake as I had heard stories from my dad, but I had yet to catch one. Not knowing how to distinguish one fish from another, and only having heard stories of the bass, I surmised that the large fish circling about ten feet in front of me was a bass.

I was mesmerized, trying to guess which direction it would turn and if it was the biggest fish in the lake or if there were bigger ones. I stepped to the edge of the dock to get a closer look, and as I did, I was surprised that the fish started swimming towards me rather than away. It headed right for me as if to torpedo the posts supporting the dock, but instead of going into a post it swam between the two posts that held up the board that I was standing on. Transfixed by curiosity I continued to follow the fish with my eyes, not fully realizing that they were connected to my head which was now no longer centered above my feet but peering over the edge of the dock in order to keep the fish in view. As I continued to lean forward to keep sight of the fish swimming beneath my feet, my aunts and uncles were suddenly distracted from their card game by a giant splash, which of course was me falling into the lake fully clothed with my paddle and life jacket. They called down to me to see if I was okay. Aside from being soaked and embarrassed, I was fine, but I could not figure out how to explain to them why I fell off a perfectly stationary dock into the water.

You may be thinking I deserve a pass on this. I was only seven years old after all, but the truth is I could go on with stories like these well into my thirties. And each story could end with "if only someone was there to...." Perhaps this was the lesson I was learning and one of the reasons I finally decided to get married. Being married is like always having that person standing by you, seeing that you are about to fall off the dock into the water, and is ready to grab you before you do. They are there to watch the horizon while you are looking at the ground. While I take comfort in knowing Julie will be there looking out for me, I need to be mindful of playing the role of the watchful friend, too. Learning the answer to Antonio's riddle was a metaphor for the decision I was making to get married. For me, anyways, it is best to walk with a friend. And how I met that friend...how I met Julie...well, keep reading.

The Confession

In truth, my journey along the Camino started not in Roncesvalles, but a year earlier, in Philadelphia. It was there where the mystical seeds for making the pilgrimage were first planted. At thirty-six years old, I was still quite the bachelor. Now, before you start making judgements, let me explain what I mean by this because I realize that there are many different definitions for the term "quite the bachelor." I had my own apartment. I didn't have to consult anyone when I wanted to go play golf, or play poker on a Friday night, or feel guilty if the main entrée for dinner was a bowl of cereal, again. And I had dated a bit, but I never had a relationship that lasted more than six months.

It's possible that I was afraid of relationships, having witnessed first-hand with my parents how bad relationships could be, but I wasn't opposed to the idea of marriage in general. In fact, I had just been asked to be the best man in my friend Randy's wedding that year. He had been dating his bride for a couple of years, and when she told him he had better pop the question soon if they were going to stay together, he did. I could tell he was very happy, and looking forward to starting a family. I arranged the bachelor party, delivered the best man speech, and met a particularly interesting bridesmaid. Not too long after the wedding Randy called me to tell me that the particularly interesting bridesmaid was recently single and set me up on a date. It was a long distance set up, so we had to pick a weekend when we could travel and actually meet up in person. We picked a weekend after Easter.

Now the week before Easter was Holy Week, and it was usually the only time of year that I would actually go to confession, and even then, I would sometimes skip that particular sacrament. But there was something calling me that year to go, even though I couldn't put my finger on exactly what it was. Now I wouldn't consider myself a particularly sinful person. Sure, I had my faults and shortcomings, but my conscience was clear of any of the big ones. In fact, except for the big ones, like the killing and the stealing, I wasn't entirely sure I could name the other sins. I had heard of the seven deadly sins, and the Ten Commandments. So …which was it… seven or ten? And where could I go to find the list, so I could review it to make sure I had actually committed a sin so that I could make a good confession? I rummaged through my books that I was storing in some old milk crates that made them easier to move, which was important, since I moved nine times since I graduated from college. I found the bible I got when I became a Catholic back in my junior year. After a bit of page turning, I found the chapter and verse that listed the Ten Commandments and reviewed each one carefully. I found it...the sin I would confess.

I had just moved to an apartment in the Chestnut Hill area of Philadelphia, and this was my first holiday at Our Mother of Consolation Parish. I didn't know as I was entering the church if this was one of the traditional parishes that had the little phone-booth-type confessionals where you kneel down and a little secret door slides open with an anonymous voice from the other side, that for all you know, could be God talking to you, or one of the more modern parishes where you sit down with the priest in some comfortable chairs as if about to have a few beers and talk about last Sunday's football game. OMC (that's what all the parishioners called the Our Mother of Consolation parish) was somewhere in the middle.

There were two priests listening to confession. One was off to the side out of sight from those waiting in the pews for their turn to confess. This priest I did not recognize, probably one brought in just to handle the confessions during that busy time. The other was Father Mike, who was seated in a cushioned chair in the front with another chair facing him for face-to-face confessions. I decided to get in line for Father Mike, mostly because he was familiar, but also because his line was shorter.

As I waited in the pews for my turn, I realized that Father Mike did not pick the most private place in the church for this, what I would consider a somewhat personal sacrament. The chairs were right there in front of everyone in the middle where the acoustics of the church carried the murmurings of the confession discussion back to the pews where those of us who were waiting could hear. And it's not that I was trying to eavesdrop, but if you listened carefully, you could almost make out what was being said. Well, I, not wanting to invade on anyone's privacy, diverted my attention to the back of the church to focus on my own thoughts. I also wanted to focus on the entrance to the door, because at that point, I was the last in line for confession and if no one else came in, I wouldn't have to worry about anyone listening in on my sins. It was finally my turn.

I did the quick look around and sighed in relief, as I saw the pews behind me empty. I walked up to Father Mike, said hello, made the sign of the cross and said, "Forgive me Father for I have sinned. It has been about a year since my last confession. I have been coveting my neighbor's wife."

As the words escaped my mouth, and I saw Father Mike's

eyes widen with concern, I realized, that wasn't exactly what I meant.

"Well, not actually the wife of the guy who lives next door to me," I corrected myself.

Father Mike's expression turned slightly from his warm understanding face to a subtly squinted look of confusion, as he wasn't quite sure where I was going with this.

"What I mean to say is that many of my friends are married, and before I really get myself in trouble here, it's not that I am coveting any of their wives either. It's just that I see the happiness that many of them have, and wish that I could find someone that I could share my life with and share that kind of happiness, too."

I went on to tell him that I didn't really know how to characterize this sin, so the "coveting" line was the only one that seemed to fit. I also explained that I did not feel badly towards any of my friends, just felt a little jealous at times, not of the particular person, but of the relationship, which made me feel a little empty inside.

Father Mike was probably not much older than I was and looked like he could have been the center for his college basketball team based on his height and build. He had a very calm demeanor and talked like an average guy even when he was giving his homily. He was the kind of priest who seemed to relate to the lives of his parishioners and was not one of these older, judgmental, balding fellows with a holier-than-thou air about them. No, Father Mike seemed pretty cool, which was probably another reason I chose his confessional line.

After listening to my confession, he said it sounded like I had a good understanding of myself and that I seemed to have a good head on my shoulders. He suggested that I pray on it and ask God to help me find what it was that I was looking for. He sent me off with the typically prescribed three Hail Marys, and a sense that I was not doomed to the shallow unfulfilling kind of relationships that I had had until then.

Confession is a funny sacrament. It conjures up this image of a mystical get out of jail free card, as if you can commit any kind of misdeed and then as long as you go tell a priest about it, poof, everything is good again. I don't see it this way. The sacraments, as I understand them, are ways that we as human beings connect with God.

As a Roman Catholic, I have learned of seven sacraments and each one is a different touch point we have with Jesus as we journey through life. The sacraments of initiation (Baptism, Confirmation, and Eucharist) are there to help us start our journey and sustain us along the way. The sacraments of healing (Penance and Anointing the Sick) are there to help us when we need help or we stray off course. The sacraments of service (Matrimony and Holy Orders) are there to help us decide what course to chart and how to better serve others. And, of course, the sacrament of Last Rites when our journey on earth comes to an end.

As I reflect on my story of walking the Camino de Santiago, it is interesting to see how different sacraments have played a pivotal role in my journey. But the one that I feel was particularly life changing for me was penance, or confession. When I walked into the church that week before Easter, I was not going in to wipe some slate of misdeeds clean. I went in knowing that something in my life was not going well and that what I was struggling with was some kind of spiritual dissonance. The act of making a confession forced me to put into words and try to express out loud the issue with which I was struggling. That act alone, of just formulating my confession, put me on the track to dealing with it. Participating in the sacrament of penance helped me transform that dissonance into resonance. Resonance is explained by Richard Rohr, a Franciscan priest and author of books on spirituality, in this way:

> "The traditional and most universal word to describe a different access to truth was simply "to pray about something." But that lovely word "prayer" has been so deadened by pious use and misuse that we now have to describe this different mental attitude with new words. I am going to introduce a different word here, so you can perceive prayer in a fresh way, and perhaps appreciate what we mean by contemplation. The word is "resonance." Prayer is actually setting out a tuning fork. All you can really do in the spiritual life is get tuned to receive the always present message. Once you are tuned, you will receive, and it has nothing to do with worthiness or the group you belong to, but only inner resonance and a capacity for mutuality. The Sender is absolutely and always present and broadcasting; the only change is with the receiver station." (Rohr, The Naked Now, p. 101-2)

I did not fully grasp this concept of prayer when I went to confession that day, but as I look back on it, I realize the sacrament of penance is acknowledging that your tuning fork is out of tune and needs to be reset and doing penance is trying to make the needed adjustments. I don't know if there is anything magical about the three Hail Marys I said as the penance Father Mike prescribed, but I have no doubt I was more clearly receiving the broadcasts when I left the church. As I walked back to my apartment, making a left on Germantown Ave. at the top of Chestnut Hill and ambling back to Highland pondering my confession, I was not expecting to get an answer to my prayers as quickly as I did.

The Table in London

It was not two days later when I got an e-mail from my cousin Joanna from Boston asking me to show a friend of hers around Philly while she was there for a conference. I really didn't think much of it. First of all, I was too focused on just the surprise of hearing from Joanna, because I usually only see her once every couple of years at some family function like a wedding or the annual family picnic if we both happen to make it. Secondly, I was never that astute when it came to subtlety in messages. I just wrote back and told her I would be happy to show her friend around. Of course I would do a favor for my cousin. That's what family is for. And then, like the last person in the room to get a joke, it hit me. My cousin was trying to set me up on a blind date. So, I called her that night to clarify things. I told her I would be happy to show her friend around, but that in case this was a set-up, she should know that I already had a plan to meet that bridesmaid that I had met at my friend's wedding, so I wasn't looking for another set-up at the moment.

My cousin said that it was not a set-up, but just a friend of hers who was going to be in a city for a few days, a city she wasn't familiar with, where she didn't know anyone, and thought it would be nice to have someone show her around. She gave me her name and cell phone number. For those of you who have been keeping up with my meandering story so far, you have probably already figured this one out. My cousin's friend's name was Julie.

Now Julie was only going to be in town from Tuesday to Thursday, so there weren't a lot of options in terms of getting together. In fact, I already had two of those nights scheduled with school related functions, (I was a high school teacher, which I think I mentioned already), so only Wednesday was good. I called her number to let her know when would be good with me and if she were available. As to be expected, I got her voicemail recording. I must say, though, that I was immediately intrigued by her raspy, late-night-radio-DJ voice. It was very warm and confident. She returned my call, and of course, got my voicemail. We played phone tag a couple of times, and I was beginning to feel that we were not going to be able to get together. When we finally talked, it was already Wednesday night, and too late to meet up. Thursday night I was supposed to go to some seminar in the evening for which I could get in-service credit, something you needed in Pennsylvania to keep your teaching license. I decided that it was so uncommon that my cousin called to ask a favor, that it would be the better part of valor to blow off the seminar, so I planned to pick Julie up after dinner at her hotel for a tour of the city and a couple of drinks.

I arranged to pick her up at her hotel by the airport. I walked in the lobby and called her cell phone to let her know I was there. And there was that voice, calm, reassured, but with a slight bit of excitement that made me think she was glad I came. I browsed the tourist kiosk with all the Philadelphia brochures as I waited for her elevator to come down. I must have got caught up in the sightseeing suggestions, because the next thing I know I hear that voice right behind me, "Adam?"

And with all my charm and savvy that I had practiced time and again on all my prior dates, I summoned the muse of suave openers and responded with, "Julie?"

OK, I know it wasn't very inspired, but I was disarmed immediately when we made eye contact. These warm reassuring brown eyes, looked right through me as if to say, "Relax, you don't need to try to impress me, I'm just glad you're here."

We got in my Jeep. I made certain to walk around to the passenger side to open up the door for her. This act of chivalry seemed almost misplaced as climbing into a Jeep is so awkward, that maintaining an air of grace and manners would be better substituted for a stepladder or at least a boost. Julie didn't skip a beat and hopped right in. I gave her what I like to call the five-dollar tour of Philadelphia. We drove down South Street to Old City, past the waterfront up to Elfreth's Alley, down Market Street to the Liberty Bell and Independence Hall, back down Market, past the Declaration House to City Hall, around Love Park to the Benjamin Franklin Parkway, down the avenue of the flags, passing the Rodin Museum and up and around the Art Museum. Now, you have to get out at the Art Museum to do the compulsory jog up the Rocky Steps. And the view from the top of the steps is pretty impressive. Then if you walk to the back of the museum there is a little gazebo overlooking the Schuylkill River and Boathouse Row.

If this is done in the evening, Boathouse Row is particularly impressive as the eves and windows of the boathouses are outlined with white lights transforming the little buildings into a magical skyline reflecting off the river. Now ending the tour up at the Art Museum was perfect, because you are in the Fairmount area of the city where you can find a lot of pubs and restaurants. I had been to a few of them, but I had just read a review of a pub called the Bishop's Collar that said it was a trendy nightspot where many of the locals gather for a good beer and some pub food. What I didn't know was that there was a Flyers game on TV that night, thus turning this trendy nightspot into a jam-packed fan fury of diehards cheering for their team at the top of their lungs. Not the best place to sit for a drink and some idle chat.

Fortunately, I remembered this other place down the street called London. It was also a pretty hip spot with a neon champagne class, bubbles and the name London illuminated on the side of this brick storefront. A few café tables with umbrellas outside and the view of the old Eastern State Penitentiary, which was now just a big stone museum in the center of the city that was illuminated at night and made it look like a castle. This pub had the right feel for an alternative to the Bishop's Collar. We walked in and found a high round table with bar stools in the corner by the window. Perfect.

The interior of London had an old pressed tin ceiling, dark wood throughout, and lighting that made the bar a very cozy spot. A waitress came over to take our order. I asked Julie what she wanted, and she asked what kind of beer they had. A subtle smile came to my face, as I was relieved that she was the beer drinking sort and not one to put on airs by ordering a Cosmopolitan or one of the trendy new "chick-tinis." She asked me about this Yuengling Beer, not having heard of it up in Boston.

I explained that Yuengling is America's oldest brewery and a pretty popular beer in the Philly area. We ordered two Yuenglings, and as they arrived, I found that we were in the middle of a conversation as if we were two old friends who were catching up after not seeing each other for a while.

Again, I had this uncontrollable smile come over my face. I was hoping she did not notice, because I didn't know if I could have explained really why I was smiling. We talked for a while, only being interrupted a few times by a violinist who was roaming from table to table taking requests, and would play anything from Vivaldi to AC/DC! I'll admit this was odd entertainment, but it made for good conversation. Truth be told, the conversation was already good, so maybe it was just odd.

Anyway, we really opened up with each other at that table in London. She told me about her previous marriage and how she had finally decided after six years of trying to make things work out with an alcoholic husband, to get divorced. She had moved with him to England, thinking this was another chance to make a fresh start, but drinking binges continued, and after five months in London, she flew back home alone to Boston. That was the end of her marriage, which was now four years ago. I knew she was divorced, because my cousin had mentioned it, but I was surprised she was sharing so much personal information with me.

Usually, when someone who I just meet shares really personal information like that, I am put off a bit. There are unwritten rules about what you can talk about, when and with whom. The spectrum runs from meaningless small talk to spilling your guts, and you only cross the line from one category to the next depending on the closeness of a relationship. You don't spill your guts to someone on line with you at the supermarket checkout, and you don't have meaningless small talk with your best friend. When you meet someone for the first time, conversation usually stays at the shallow end of the spectrum, and if it doesn't, it is usually very awkward. But talking with Julie didn't feel awkward at all. In fact, talking with Julie came as easily and as comfortably as kicking your feet up on the couch at home and clicking on the T.V., only more interesting and interactive.

At one point Julie got up to use the restroom and, as she was walking away from me, I caught myself thinking how cute she looked in her jeans. It wasn't until then that I remembered that I was not on a date. My actual date was not supposed to be until that coming weekend when the bridesmaid was coming to visit. I had completely forgotten about her. Not just that she was coming to visit, but I had completely forgotten about her. This unexpected evening with Julie had caught me off guard. I was just doing a favor for my cousin, and not at all thinking about "meeting someone special." After all, I had planned a weekend with the bridesmaid to see if maybe she was the "someone special." But Julie just consumed my thoughts. Who was this person who made me feel as though I had known her all my life? When would I get a chance to see her again? And why couldn't I get that silly grin off my face?

Well, the evening finished off innocently enough. On our ride back, I noticed I was low on gas, and asked her if she minded if I stopped off to fill up. I assured her that it was not the old "we ran out of gas" ploy. She smiled and said it was no problem. We continued this great conversation in the car and I finally dropped her off in front of her hotel. I offered to walk her in, but she politely declined. As she walked into the hotel, all I could think of was that she was going back to Boston the next day, and I may never see her again.

The bridesmaid arrived two days later. I really tried to give it a chance, but I just didn't feel the same way as I did when I was around Julie. When the weekend came to an end, I decided to be up front with her. I told her that I was interested in seeing someone else. I knew that it would not be hard to try to date both girls at the same time since they lived in two different cities and neither one lived in mine, but I felt something very real with Julie and I didn't want to waste time playing games. So, I made a clean break. I knew I made the right decision, but the truth was, I didn't even know if Julie was interested in seeing me again. What was the next step? I figured I would use the same tack as most twenty-first century romances, and start with an email. I sent her off an email telling her what a great time I had meeting her and tried to keep it casual by following up with a, "So, let's go out for a beer again some time, oh yeah, you live in Boston." Truthfully, I didn't know what to expect. Long distance relationships are very difficult to maintain, but they're even harder to start. But I hit the send button, anyway, and figured I'd let the chips fall where they may. I didn't have to wait long in anticipation. I got a reply the next day.

"Maybe we can meet in New York," she suggested. "I'm going to a friend's wedding in New York City next week, and it's closer to Philly than Boston is." So, our first date was to be in New York, but I really look back at that table in London as the place where I first…well…let's just say where I first met Julie.

The Coincidences

It is a bit of a coincidence that Julie and I met in a bar called London, the same name as the city where Julie decided to leave her husband, don't you think? Julie ended one relationship in London and started a new one in a bar called London. Come on, you have to admit that is a bit weird. Anyway, the weekend of her friend's wedding arrived and I drove into New York to meet Julie. It was a rainy Saturday in Manhattan so we decided to visit the Hayden Planetarium and then go find a place for lunch. It was a fun morning walking around New York, and the drizzle gave us a reason to get close under my umbrella. I remember her holding on to my arm as we walked. I could have stayed under that umbrella with her all morning. I can't really explain it, but the way she held my arm just made me feel really close to her. Ironically, I didn't need the words to explain it.

The words I was looking for were in big bold letters hanging on a giant banner in front of this Central Park West building we were about to pass: "Jules Rules." I looked at her and signaled to the banner above us. "Jules" of course is the nickname for Julie that her family and friends use. She also used "Jules" as part of her email address. We both looked at each other with a grin and a twinkle of the eye as if we just agreed to take part in some schoolyard prank. We felt compelled to go in.

It was some exhibit by the New York Historical Society

about some artist named Jules Something-or-other. Neither of us really cared much about the exhibit, but I could not get over the irony that just when I had this feeling about Julie I couldn't put into words, there they were on an enormous banner hanging across the very sidewalk we were walking on. "Jules Rules."

We walked back out into the rain just long enough to duck into a corner restaurant for some lunch. Once we shook ourselves dry and found a place to store the umbrella, we sat down and a waiter came up to take our drink order. Julie unhesitatingly ordered a hot chocolate. Now this caught me by surprise. "Who orders a hot chocolate in a New York restaurant?" I thought. But it was perfect. It was just what you needed on a day like that, and instead of Julie conforming to some drink etiquette or trend, she ordered what the moment required. She had such an aura of contentment and ease about her that I couldn't help but get caught up in it. I wasn't thinking about being in New York City, or seeing the sights, or fighting with the crowds, or getting soaked by the rain or knowing what to order in a restaurant. I was just thinking about Julie and how much I was enjoying just being with her. We talked and laughed as we ate, and the Big Apple outside the restaurant window somehow disappeared into that cup of hot chocolate. I was definitely falling for this girl.

She had to leave to get ready for the wedding, so I dropped her off back in front of the apartment. As she got out, there was that awkward moment about how to part, and if I was going to kiss her or not. As the awkward moment grew, and the car horns beeped, the chance for a kiss was gone, but I told her I would love to see her again, and she agreed. That was enough to make up for the missed kiss opportunity.

Emails became phone calls, and phone calls became road

trips. And as my teaching profession afforded me some free time during the summer months, the road trips became longer and more often. I remember my first road trip to visit Julie when I stayed with her at her parents' house. This was the house where she grew up in Massachusetts.

It was a brown Dutch colonial on a quiet suburban street with a third-floor addition built on to accommodate all seven kids in her family. When I arrived, I discovered that her parents were away and none of the other siblings were living there as they were all grown and had moved out. I must admit, I felt a bit like a teenager again, wondering if the parents knew I was coming and would be staying unchaperoned in their house. Julie was very proper in showing me the room I would be staying in on the second floor, which was distinctly different from her old bedroom on the third floor where she was staying. Now, keeping in mind we had not even kissed yet, sharing a room would have been a bit presumptuous. I did need to remedy that problem of not having a first kiss.

Recognizing the awkwardness of being in her parents' house, I suggested she and I go out for an evening walk on the nearby beach. We drove down to Deveraux Beach, which was only a few blocks away. It was a pebbly beach with a little bit of sand with a public pavilion for picnics, a small playground and a snack bar called Lime Rickey's. We got out of the car and started our beach stroll. It was dark now, and there was nobody else on the beach with us.

While this beach faced the Atlantic Ocean, the waves rolling in that night were lapping up on the shore providing a melodic rhythm to our stroll. As we walked, she grabbed my arm and held onto it like she did when we were walking in New York City on our "first date." It was a warm night with a bit of a breeze coming off the water, and the sky was clear and the moon was full. Taking advantage of the setting that nature had presented, I pointed up to the moon and asked her if she had ever seen the Rabbit in the Moon before. This was an image I had learned about from Mexican folklore that is simply a different way of looking at the Man in the Moon, so I thought it might be novel to Julie and entice her to look up at it.

As she tilted her head upwards, that was when I went in for the kiss. Our lips met effortlessly, and she held her pose as if she had been expecting such a move. It was a great first kiss. As we both drew back and looked at each other smiling, I felt such a sigh of relief that the first kiss was everything I hoped it would be: innocent yet romantic, gentile yet firm enough to maintain the moment, and alluring in all the right ways that we both went in for the second one. It was a perfect moment on a moonlit night. Now, every time I hear Van Morrison's song "Moondance," I think of that night on Deveraux Beach and our first kiss.

By the end of the summer, Julie had rented this small apartment in the Back Bay area of Boston and invited me to come up for the week. While the apartment was in a great location for getting around Boston, there was one thing it lacked that every apartment in Boston should have during the summer... air conditioning. It was excessively hot and humid that week.

One day I suggested we go see a movie in the afternoon. Julie asked what I wanted to see, and I told her it didn't matter. I just wanted to spend a few hours inside an air-conditioned movie theater. So, we walked to the nearest theater and decided we would see whatever movie was playing. The next showing was a film called "Alex and Emma," which was a movie I had not even heard of, but I could tell by the title it was going to be a sappy little romantic comedy. But my need for atmospheric comfort outweighed my desire for genuine entertainment, so we bought tickets and went in.

As the plot of the movie unfolds, we are introduced to a guy writing a story about a character named Adam who lives in Boston and has a gambling problem. The writer enlists the help of a woman from Philadelphia as a stenographer. OK, this was weird; a guy named Adam, the Boston-Philadelphia connection, and the gambling problem? You see, when Julie and I first started dating, she said she thought I was great, but there must be something wrong with me. Apparently, any guy who is still single in his mid-thirties must have some neurosis, or skeletons in the closet, or flaw that has kept him from getting married.

Now within the first month of our dating, I coincidentally went to both Atlantic City and Las Vegas. That was the first time I had ever been to Las Vegas, and even though Atlantic City is a short drive from Philly, I would go maybe twice a year with sixty bucks in my pocket, so I could hardly be considered to have had a gambling problem. But Julie needed to find some chink in my armor, and so jokingly, she decided that it must be a secret gambling problem. So, sitting in that theater, I found it very bizarre that we just happen upon a movie that has two characters that are falling in love, one from Boston, one from Philadelphia, and the guy's name is Adam, with a gambling problem.

I turn to Julie and ask her suspiciously, "Are you sure you didn't know what this movie was about?"

But I knew she hadn't planned it, because it was my suggestion to go see the earliest movie playing at the closest theater, and it just happened to be this one.

There were other strange coincidences that summer. While I was home alone on my couch watching an episode of Law and Order, missing Julie, I hear Detective Lenny Briscoe interviewing witnesses at the crime scene of some boating accident. The witness tells the detective that the only people on the boat were him and his girlfriend, his friend Adam, and Adam's girlfriend Julie. I did a double take, because I couldn't believe I heard on TV the words "Adam and his girlfriend Julie" just as I was thinking about missing Julie. Weird.

Then there was the time when Julie was visiting me in Philadelphia and we were driving in the car listening to 88.5 WXPN on the radio. This is a public radio station out of the University of Pennsylvania that plays a great mix of music. Now it is not uncommon for this station to play a song I have never heard before, but the words of this particular new song caught my attention.

The chorus kept repeating "Hey Julie" and then I heard, "Sometimes I catch myself staring into space, counting down the hours 'til I get to see your face." And it continues, "How did it come to be that you and I must be far away from each other every day?" The song ends with a repeating, "Julie, I swear, it's so hard to bear it and I'd never make it through without you around." Then the DJ came on to say the name of the song was "Hey Julie" written by a guy from New Jersey named Adam. OK, is this too much of a coincidence?

I grew up in New Jersey. Julie and I are driving along in a car while she is visiting all the way from Boston listening to a song by a guy named Adam singing about a girl named Julie without whom he can't get along and how he thinks about her even though she is far away. Weird. I find out the song is by a group called Fountains of Wayne, and I promptly go out and by the album. Needless to say, I played it ad nauseum until the words were committed to memory.

As the summer came to an end, we had to settle for only seeing each other on the weekends. Now Julie was great about chasing down a cheap fare on Air Tran out of Boston, and came down to see me quite a bit. I was feeling a bit guilty, because she was doing more of the traveling now, and spending money on flights. I was glad to see her, don't get me wrong, but I just felt guilty...I don't know...maybe it's that I am more traditional than I thought, and felt that the guy should pay for stuff and do all the courting. Each time she came, I was just as excited as the first.

I would always park and go in and meet her in the airport. Since 9/11, the airport security wouldn't let anyone without a ticket go to the gate, so I had to settle for waiting outside the security check. Julie insisted that she could just call me on my cell phone when she arrived, and I could just pick her up at the curb, but for me, it took all the fun out of it. I loved looking down the corridor as the passengers walked towards all of us waiting ...trying to get the first glimpse of her. I could always pick out her walk even before I could see her face. She has a distinctive little bounce in her step that sets her apart from everyone else, and it brings a smile to my face every time I see it. As she got closer, I could see her smiling, and then I would start to smile even more. I would give her a big hug and kiss, take her bag and we would walk together to the car sharing stories of the flight or the traffic, as if it were the biggest adventure in the world.

During one visit, I got tickets to see a Peter Gabriel concert at the Tweeter Center, which is this open-air venue on the Jersey side of the Delaware River overlooking the Philly skyline. We took the ferry across the river and walked to the concert with our blankets and a tarp we had bought that afternoon at Target, planning for the grass to be a little wet. We had lawn seats. There was also a possibility of a shower that night, and I thought the tarp would make a good shelter. Well, not only did the rain hold off, but the moon came out and we could see the stars above us as we listened to the concert.

As we lied down on the blankets looking up at the night sky, I pointed out different constellations I remembered learning as a kid, and we saw Venus in the sky. I asked Julie if she knew how to tell the difference between a star and a planet. She said she didn't, although she could have just been being nice and letting me continue to try to impress her with my extremely limited repertoire of astronomy. I told her that if it twinkles, then it is a star, and if it doesn't, then it's a planet. Truth be told, I wasn't sure if it was Venus or Mars we saw, but I like to think it was the goddess of love looking down on us that night.

Then the song began. It was In Your Eyes. As we kissed there on the blanket under the stars, I felt like I was back in high school. It was the thrill of that young romance, yet it was deep. It reminded me of John Cusack holding the boom box over his head in the movie "Say Anything," as he tried to win back the girl he loved. It was a great moment. I knew by then that I had fallen in love with Julie, but I was not ready to tell her. It may have been fear of her not feeling the same way, or simply fear of saying the words out loud. I had never felt that way before, and was a little afraid of how the words would sound. And once those words are out, there is no taking it back. I mean, if you tell someone you love her, there it is. Commitment. The big C. What every guy is afraid of.

Julie also had some commitment issues having been through a very difficult marriage of six years. Since her divorce she had dated other guys, but nothing serious. We swapped stories of former girlfriends and boyfriends. It's funny how names get forgotten and replaced with "the old guy who would never tell me his age" or "the psycho chick who gave me a copy of Men are from Mars and Women are from Venus to read as a homework assignment" and various other names that better describe your memory of past romances than real names ever could.

Now the difference between Julie and I, was that all of the names in my stories had been forgotten, but there was one name in Julie's past that she could not forget. It was the name of her first husband. They had dated since college, got married, and were together for six years. Now I didn't have a problem with the fact that she was married before. It may have been because I was so into her, or that I had learned from my dad, who had been on his third marriage, that you can find the right person even if you had trouble the first couple of times figuring that out. But Julie was having trouble trusting again. She told me she started seeing a therapist after the divorce, and that for years, she was not ready to open herself up again emotionally to another person.

I was impressed that Julie was taking action to get her life back on track. In addition to talking with her therapist, to work out some issues, she also decided to travel the world for a year. So, she quit her job, talked her older brother Jimmy into joining her, and headed off to South America to begin her sojourn. She shared many of her adventures with me, and in addition to learning that she had a very free and adventurous spirit, I also realized Julie was opening up to me. She shared stories of her travels, like her climb to Macchu Picchu, her African Safari, and her sixteen-day trek in Nepal. And when she finished traversing the globe, she stopped in Spain on her way back for a month-long course in Spanish. She was there by herself in Madrid.

I am not sure what it was exactly that inspired her to hang out in Spain that summer, but I can't help think about another strange coincidence. I was in Spain, by myself, that very same summer. I was taking part of a course for teachers at the University of Santiago de Compostela. Before arriving in Santiago, I spent a few days with my friend Antonio in Madrid, and I often wonder if Julie and I might have passed on the street or in some tapas bar before we ever knew each other. "Coincidences are not accidents, but signals from the universe which can guide us toward our true destiny," according to Deepak Chopra. "When you live your life with an appreciation of coincidences and their meanings, you connect with the underlying field of infinite possibilities. This is when the magic begins." (Chopra, p. 12).

So, what was I to make of all these coincidences? Were they signals from the universe guiding me towards Julie? I believe they were. And the magic was about to begin.

The Ring and the Fiery Mountain

This part of my tale has nothing to do with hobbits or wizards despite what the title may imply, but it does include some magical moments. And, I must admit, there are some parallels between my story and that of Frodo Baggins. Both are tales about long journeys on foot, secretly carrying a ring, and a life-changing event at a volcano. In my story, however, what happens with the ring and the volcano precedes the long journey, the journey along the Camino. This is the story of how Julie and I got engaged.

We had only been together for a few months, but Julie and I had conversations about relationships, marriage, and having kids. These conversations were never in terms of each other, however. They were always hypothetical, or so I thought. One weekend we decided to visit the quaint Victorian town of Cape May and while driving down in the car, the question came up, "If you were to get married, what kind of a wedding would you want?"

I think she brought up the question, because she had been married already, so if it were my question, it would have been, "if you were to get married again...." I told her that I would want something big, but less traditional. I wanted to get married in a Catholic church, but the reception should be more like a happy hour at a bar or a clambake on the beach than a formal reception.

I told her I wanted a big wedding so that there would be enough people in attendance so that my parents would not have to interact with each other. You see, my parents were divorced, which I think I mentioned, but not happily so, and, even after twenty-five years of being apart, they still didn't get along with each other. In fact, the disdain they had for one another seemed to continue to simmer over the years, only to roll into a boil from time to time.

To avoid them rolling into a full boil at my sister's wedding, my task was to run interference, so that my dad wouldn't hear my mom mention how old she thought he looked, or that my mom wouldn't hear my dad comment on the "spiker" she had hanging from her nose. Yes, both of those comments were made during the rehearsal dinner. I also had to do shuttle diplomacy with my aunts and uncles during the reception so that they could visit with my mom or dad without feeling like they were betraying their family by cavorting with the enemy. It was ridiculous, but it was a full-time job for me to make sure that they did not ruin my sister's wedding. This was just one of many times when I was grateful to have an older sister, who paved the way through life's unforeseen pitfalls, so that I might have a chance to avoid them.

So, in thinking about my own wedding, I knew I needed to have a big venue and invite enough people so that my parents could be entertained throughout the event without ever having to cross paths. Julie said she wanted a small ceremony with just immediate family and close friends. Since this line of questioning had already been opened, I decided to press a little further.

"If someone were to propose to you," I asked, "what kind of ring would you want?"

She paused for a moment, and I could tell she was really pondering this question as if she had not even thought about it before.

"I don't know," she replied, "but I wouldn't want a diamond ring."

Now Julie never wore much jewelry, usually just a black leather Swiss Army watch and some small silver loop earrings. When she said it wasn't her style...it just wasn't her, I knew she was being sincere. And that was the extent of our conversation about marriage. We never talked about it again.

But a few months later, I found myself thinking about a ring. I hadn't actually talked to Julie about us getting married, which I guess would have been the safer course of action to take before buying a ring. Nevertheless, I set about looking for one, only knowing that she didn't want a diamond. On the one hand, this is every guy's dream...not having to plunk three months' salary down on a piece of jewelry. But on the other hand, if not a diamond, then what?

After some browsing in local jewelry stores with little success, I decided to expand the search to the Internet. I came across a jewelry store in the western part of Ireland where the Claddagh ring tradition supposedly started. The symbol of the hands clasping a heart topped by a crown represents friendship, love and loyalty. This had the perfect sentiment. What is a marriage without these three?

I had seen traditional Claddagh rings before, but there was this one ring that was very unique. It was a white gold band with the Claddagh symbol in the middle where a stone would be. The band had tiny diamonds embedded on either side of the heart, hands and crown. It was just enough to give it a sparkle detail, but yet it didn't look like a "diamond ring." It was delicate and unique while understated. This was perfect.

So, I set about getting Julie's ring size by casually removing a ring she wore on her ring finger and putting it on my pinky to see where it would come down to. I did this a few times to make sure I had the right measurement. Julie didn't suspect anything. She thought I kept doing this because this was the ring that she had made from melting down her first wedding ring after she got divorced. She thought the symbolism of the ring bothered me, like it was some kind of reminder of a past love. This wasn't the case at all; I just wanted to get her ring size without her knowing what I was up to. I then went to a local jeweler and tried on their sizing rings to find out her size. She was a five and a half.

It took a couple of months, but the ring finally arrived. I was excited, but nervous. What if she didn't like it? I had to show it to someone to get some feedback, so I invited my friends Kirk and Corinne over to inspect the object of my future happiness. Kirk and Corinne were one of the aforementioned couples whose relationship I coveted. I not only enjoyed hanging out with them and trusted their opinion, but Corinne was also an art teacher who made jewelry, so she would be a particularly good source for an opinion on such matters. I got the thumbs up on the ring, so all that was left now was how to pop the question.

As I mentioned, Julie and I had never talked about getting married. Sure, we had that conversation on the way to Cape May, but that was just a hypothetical "If you were ever to..." kind of conversation. So, me buying a ring was a bit of a risk. Not only had we not talked about getting married, neither one of us had actually said those three words that are so difficult to introduce into a relationship... "I love you." In fact, it wasn't until Thanksgiving, when Julie and I flew out to California to spend the holiday with my mom, that the words were lovingly pried out of my mouth.

My mom had been living in Southern California for a few years now to be closer to my sister, and I thought visiting for the holiday would be a good opportunity for her to get to know Julie. Julie survived what I can only call hazing by my mother. She invited us to play Hearts, my mom loved playing cards, only to hiss at Julie when she had to take thirteen points when Julie dropped the queen of spades on her. While chatting with Julie out by the pool of her apartment complex, my mom almost nonchalantly dropped the line, "I hope Adam meets someone nice someday." Really. That is what she said to the woman whom I just flew out to California to meet her, whom I was clearly presenting as "the someone nice" I wanted to be with. My mom always had a way of slipping in some seemingly innocent zingers.

But Julie took it in stride and just continued being pleasant with my mom. The second night of our visit, while sleeping on the trundle bed in the den, I rolled over to Julie and kissed her, looked into her eyes and said,

"I think I…I'm …I think I'm… falling for you."

She could tell I was having trouble finding the words. She looked back at me and, with a knowing grin and a sparkle in her eye, she asked,

"You mean you love me?"

And there they were. The words I knew I felt but couldn't seem to say out loud.

"Yeah, I love you."

Ahhh. That felt kind of nice. That wasn't that hard after all. Julie smiled at me and said,

"I love you, too."

She made that whole exchange that I was so struggling with in my head so easy and so natural. It was as if we both just put words to what we already knew, so there was nothing uncomfortable about it. I mean, I knew I already loved her. I bought her a ring already for Christ's sake.

Why was saying, "I love you," such a challenge? "I love you" was not a phrase used much in my family growing up, and when it was used, I often didn't trust the sentiment. I didn't always see the love, what with the way my parents fought, and then the way my sister and I often ended up as expendable pawns in the feuding that continued after the divorce. "Love" became a word that felt contrived. You knew you were supposed to say it, but it didn't come naturally. But here I was with Julie, and she taught me how to say those three words in such a gentle way as if reintroducing me to an old friend. And once that old friend was back in my life, "I love you," just seemed to slip out a lot more easily and a lot more often.

We said we loved each other. Check. I bought a ring. Check. But I still had to figure out a way to ask her to marry me. I soon learned that Julie's younger sister was studying in Costa Rica that year, and her family was going down over Christmas vacation to visit her. Julie asked if I would like to go with them. According to Julie, non-family members were not customarily allowed on such trips, but her parents, for some reason, agreed to her request that I join her. That was it. That was the opportunity I was looking for. I would propose while we were in Costa Rica.

One concern I had was bringing the ring through airport security. What would happen if the box with the ring in it set off a metal detector and I would have to explain what was inside? Proposing in the middle of an airport security line was not my idea of romantic, but I had to take the risk. I packed the ring deep in my luggage, held my breath as it was scanned, and to my relief, my ring secretly boarded the plane without incident. Another concern I had was what if she said no. We had never talked about us getting married except for that brief hypothetical conversation on the way to Cape May, so there was no guarantee she would accept my proposal.

Furthermore, if she said no, I would be stuck there in a foreign country for a week surrounded by her whole family. That would be awkward. So, I came up with a plan. I would wait until the end of the week, so that if she said no, I would only have to suffer an uncomfortable plane ride back home. I would also figure out a way to get Julie alone, again, so that the embarrassment of being rejected would not by multiplied by having her family as witnesses. Coincidentally, her birthday fell in the middle of the week we were there, so for a birthday gift, I would get her a night stay at a lodge in the cloud forest overlooking Arenal Volcano. The night would be at the end of the week and it would be just for the two of us. That was my plan. I thought it was perfect.

Arenal was an active volcano that I had visited a number of years before on a business trip, and thought this would be the perfect place to lure her away, so I could get her alone without her suspecting anything. Now the whole family went out to dinner to celebrate her birthday in a restaurant in the town of Tamarindo, where we were staying along the coast. Earlier in the week when Julie and I were browsing the souvenir shops, we saw these puzzle boxes carved from local wood in a variety of shapes. One was the shape of a four-leaf clover. I picked it up and said,

"Does this remind you of anything?"

She smiled and nodded. She remembered our walk in the Morris Arboretum where the existence of four-leaf clovers was first put into question.

Morris Arboretum was this beautiful pastoral park in the northwestern corner of Philadelphia, where we went for a walk the first spring we met. Feeling a bit playful, I had tackled her behind a hedge where we both ended up on the ground. As we sat on the ground I started sifting through the grass with my fingers.

"What are you doing?" she asked.

"I'm looking for four-leaf clovers," I replied very matter-of-factly.

And then to my bewilderment, Julie stated,

"They don't exist."

I wasn't sure if she was speaking metaphorically about life because of her stretch of bad luck with her marriage, or if she really thought these elusive four-leafed plants were subjects of myth and legend. She insisted that there was no such thing as a four-leaf clover, to which I became obsessed with finding one to prove her wrong. I did not find one that day, but I was not going to give up.

The following week, while coaching the junior varsity softball team, I told the girls that if they found a four-leaf clover on the field during practice, they would not have to run laps. The left-fielder, whom I nicknamed "Socks" because she would often practice in her socks instead of putting on her cleats, promptly dropped to the ground and began searching with a purpose. And before I got around the infield with hitting grounders, she jumped up triumphantly shouting,

"I found one!"

Sure enough, she had found a four-leaf clover in left field, and I had the proof to show Julie that these wondrous little plants existed. And true to my word, nobody ran laps that day.

I put the wooden clover box back on the shelf and Julie and I kept meandering through the shops not really looking for anything, but rather just taking in the ambience of the little surfing village of Tamarindo. Later that day, I went back by myself, without Julie knowing, to buy the box to give to her for her birthday. The box was not really the gift. It contained the note I wrote explaining the one-night getaway. I wrapped the box and presented it to her when the whole family went out to dinner to celebrate her birthday. When she opened the box, there was a pregnant pause in conversation and I think some of her family members thought there might have been a ring inside it. I avoided making eye contact with any of them for fear of giving away my motives, even though the ring I was planning to give her was still hidden away in my luggage. Julie opened the box without hesitation showing no thoughts whatsoever of the possibility of a proposal inside. She laughed when she saw the clover box as we shared again our inside joke, and read the note in silence:

Dear Julie,

I know you don't believe in four leaf clovers, but isn't it funny how you found this box with the four-leaf clover on it? For your birthday I wish for you to find love and happiness that perhaps, before, your heart was not ready to believe in. My gift to you is a night at Volcán Arenal with a chance to see a spectacle few get to see, but more a chance to open your heart for a love that some only find once in a lifetime. To someone who helped me find a love I never thought I would find, I wish you a very happy birthday!

I LOVE YOU!
Adam

She looked at me and smiled and shared the news of our night's escape to Arenal Volcano with her family at the table. She did NOT read aloud the note to everyone, thank goodness.

The end of the week finally arrived. The Buena Vista Lodge at Arenal Volcano was truly off the beaten path. Well, actually a beaten path pretty well describes the road to get to the lodge. The two of us arrived in our rental car and decided to take an early evening tour of the cloud forest that the lodge arranged. Afterwards we made plans to have dinner at the lodge restaurant, which had a beautiful view of the volcano through panoramic windows, that opened up to the jungle for an enchanting view. The restaurant was not fancy, but it was certainly comfortable, and it offered a nice assortment of wine. It was also the only restaurant available in that part of the cloud forest, so it would have to do.

As we unpacked our bags in the room, I surreptitiously dug out the ring box from my suitcase and slipped it into my pants pocket. My heart was pounding for fear that she might see, but I was able to do it without her noticing. So, in we walked to the restaurant with the key to my future happiness hidden in my left pant pocket.

As the dinner began, everything was going smoothly. The food was good, our waiter was very friendly, and we found a nice bottle of wine to share. And just as I started to contemplate which moment to choose, or how I should ask, in walks another guest, who, from his wardrobe of a Hawaiian shirt, shorts and boat shoes, is clearly an American on vacation, with a boom box in hand. No sooner does he arrive; does he begin to engage the entire restaurant in an impromptu game of Name That Tune. He literally addressed the other tables with a wager if anyone could name the songs that he started playing on CDs he had. I could not believe what was happening! Most of the selections were seventies tunes, but I was not at all interested, as all I could think was this guy was completely ruining the atmosphere for what could very well be the most important night in my life.

Julie could see the disconcertedness in my face, and the abrupt change in my demeanor. She asked what was wrong. I said this guy was ruining a nice romantic dinner, but she assured me that she was enjoying herself and that I shouldn't worry about it. She clearly did not know what was at stake for me. I considered keeping the ring in my pocket and taking it back to Philadelphia with me until I found another more appropriate opportunity. This one was ruined.

But then, I remembered Julie had gotten a Maná CD from her sister for her birthday. This was a compact disc that had some music we both enjoyed, not to mention a few romantic tunes. It was in the rental car parked outside the restaurant. I asked her if she minded if I went to get it and ask this clown with the boom box to let us listen to it. So, I dashed out to get the CD as quickly as I could. I went up to Mr. Annoying with the boom box and explained it was my girlfriend's birthday and would he mind playing this CD she had just gotten as a gift. He agreed, and so I returned to the table to try to salvage the moment.

I was going back and forth in my mind as to whether I should go through with it now or wait for another time. As we were finishing dinner, and the waiter asked if we would like anything else, I saw my opportunity.

There was a balcony just on the other side of the panoramic windows with the same view, fresh air, and away from Mr. Annoying. So, I suggested to Julie that we get another bottle of wine, and take our glasses out to the balcony to enjoy the night sounds and sights of the volcano and the rain forest. She agreed. Out we went, and we sat on the stone railing with our feet dangling over the edge, looking out at the clouds passing over the crest of the volcano and listening to the sound of the water passing over the rocks in the creek below. Ahhh, the moment had returned. This was perfect. And just as the ring started to burn a whole in my pocket, who comes out the door to join us? None other than Mr. Annoying.

"Hey, what are you two lovebirds doing out here?" he asked, completely oblivious to the fact that we were merely trying to get away from him.

"Just enjoying the solitude of the forest and admiring the

calm and peacefulness of the volcano," I responded, trying to subtly drop a hint. He didn't get it.

"Yeah, this is a great place. I came here with my wife for our anniversary. She's wonderful." He goes on to tell us all about his wife, and how she's a dancer and a math teacher, and has so many talents and is such a wonderful person that he doesn't know why she married him. I nodded my head, not so much to show an understanding of the wonders of his wife, but more to agree that I had no idea why anyone would want to marry him.

Julie, with her unabashed charm, asked, "Well, why did she marry you?"

"Because I told her I would love her for the rest of my life," he answered. I must admit his humility was kind of endearing, but I still wanted him to leave us the hell alone.

"Well, that is quite a lot to offer," I said, letting his endearing humility get the best of me. He shrugged his shoulders and nodded his head graciously and looked back into the restaurant where his wife was sitting.

"Well, I'll leave you two love birds alone" he said with a pause afterwards, in case we invited him to stay.

Without hesitating, Julie and I both said, "OK, thanks, bye." With that he went back inside. I was beginning to think this guy was on a mission to sabotage my plans to propose. There I was, in a perfect spot, with the sounds of the cloud forest serenading us, overlooking a volcano, alone on the balcony with a bottle of wine, sitting with the woman I want to marry, and a ring hiding in its box inside my left pant pocket.

As I was trying to find the words to segue from our most recent interruption, Julie turns to me and asks,

"What about you, do you think you could love someone for the rest of your life?"

I was stunned. I couldn't believe it. There it was, like a

slow underhand pitch just lobbed up waiting for me to swing at it. Here I was trying to figure out how to ask her, and she practically popped the question herself.

So, I replied with as much confidence as I could muster, looking her right in the eye,

"Yes, I think I could." And keeping the lock I had on her and looking as deeply as I could into her soft brown eyes, I returned the question,

"And you, do you think you could love someone for the rest of your life?"

She looked at me and with a very subtle nod as if she had just reached this conclusion, she said,

"Yes, I think I could."

With that, I reached into my pocket and pulled out the box with the ring inside. When she saw what I was doing, her jaw dropped and she started to stammer,

"Wha…wait, you mean…you had…oh my…"

I interrupted, opened the box and presented the ring,

"Julie, will you marry me?"

I could tell she had no I idea I was planning on asking her to marry me. But with barely enough time to gather herself and comprehend the magnitude of the question that lay before her, she returned the deep gaze I had locked on her and with her mouth morphing from shock into an excited smile she said to me,

"Yes, I will."

Now a typical response might have been to grab her in my arms and kiss her at this moment, but my own insecurities just couldn't resist.

"Are you sure you like the ring, 'cause we can get another one…I mean I wasn't sure…I looked…"

This time Julie interrupted me by closing my lips together between her thumb and fingers, literally shutting me up and said, "It's perfect. I love it."

I put it on her finger, and it was perfect. The fit, the style, everything was perfect. More importantly, the answer was perfect. It was a perfect moment. We came together and locked in a perfect kiss as if to mark the whole thing with an exclamation point. We both were beaming. We both raised our glasses of wine and toasted to the moment.

Then, almost on cue, out walked Mr. Annoying in the Hawaiian shirt. Before he could say anything, Julie turned to him and said,

"We just got engaged!"

He halted, looked at me and looked back at her, and said, "You mean, just now? Just this minute?"

We both nodded. And in his very subtle and demure manner, he turned, walked back into the restaurant and announced it to everyone inside. While everyone was clapping, he went back to the boom box, which earlier was the bane of my evening, and put on the Maná CD to a beautiful ballad called "Vivir sin aire" and Julie and I slowed danced in each other's arms outside on the balcony.

Now you may have picked up on the detail about the second bottle of wine. So, when we woke up the next morning, and were getting ready to get to the airport to meet up with her family, I wanted to confirm that she really agreed to marry me and that it wasn't just the wine talking.

"Jules, I know we had a few glasses of wine last night, so if you aren't sure...I mean, if you..." and before I could finish my sentence, she grabbed my lips again with her fingers to shut me up and said,

"I'm sure."

When we got to the airport, she ran over to where her parents were standing at the counter while I checked the bags. I couldn't hear the conversation, but I heard later that when Julie told her mom, she responded with

"You did not, you devil!"

What I did see was that her mom gave her a big hug and then turned towards me and I could read her lips calling out across the airport check-in line,

"Welcome to the family!"

The Germans

And that is the story of how Julie and I met, fell in love, and got engaged, but it doesn't explain how we chose the Camino de Santiago as the aisle to walk down at our wedding. Remember the hypothetical conversation we had in the car on the way to Cape May that summer about what kind of wedding we would want if we ever got married? Well, it wasn't hypothetical anymore. We had to plan our wedding and we had two competing interests at work. Julie wanted a small, intimate ceremony with just family members, and I wanted a big event for all extended relatives and friends. I couldn't see any compromise to resolve our wedding dilemma. It wasn't long before Julie came up with a suggestion. She reminded me of our conversation about one of those strange coincidences that happened prior to us meeting.

Remember that Julie was in Spain taking a three-week course to learn Spanish in Madrid at the same time I was in Spain taking a course for Spanish teachers at the University of Santiago de Compostela? Well, it was taking that course when I first learned about the Camino de Santiago, or the Way of Saint James. I was intrigued by what I learned in a seminar about the history and culture of the Camino, but I was equally intrigued by the pilgrims that would walk through the town each day by the dozens to end their journey at the cathedral. They would arrive smiling, limping, singing, sunburned, alone or in a group, some on bikes, some with walking sticks, speaking languages from all parts of the world, wearing the scallop shell that identified them as pilgrims. I would see them talking with other pilgrims in the plaza and in the restaurants and bars and I would wonder about the stories they shared. I wondered what compelled all these people to make such a journey. Sure, Santiago was a fun city, full of history and tradition, with an impressive cathedral at its center, but that could be said for so many cities in the world. What was bringing so many people to this one every year? And why were so many making the trek on foot? I had decided that the only way I would really know the answers to these questions would be to make the pilgrimage myself and discover what it meant to be a pilgrim. "Someday," I thought. I told Julie about my desire to walk the Camino "someday."

"While we are still young, have the time, and don't have the commitments of a family, why don't we walk the Camino this summer when school gets out and get married at the end when we arrive in Santiago, just the two of us?" she proposed.

I thought about it for a few minutes before responding. It sounded like we would be eloping. I had never thought about eloping, but it made perfect sense. I didn't need lots of people to keep my parents separated if I didn't invite anyone at all! And if Julie's idea of small and intimate could mean just the two of us, then the wedding planning problem was solved.

"Yeah, let's do it," I agreed. And that's how my story as a pilgrim along the Camino de Santiago began. Now, if you want to go back to the very beginning of my journey, you would have to go back all the way to Germany, because that is where I was born. No, I'm not German. Apparently, to be considered a German citizen your parents have to be German, and with my dad being born in Maine, and my mom being born in New York, I didn't have an ounce of German blood in me. Although...I did need a complete blood transfusion when I was born, so maybe I did have some German blood. In any case, I was issued a birth certificate by the U.S. Embassy, so I think I could run for president if I wanted to. Don't worry, I am not planning to run for president, nor am I going to recount my life story from birth, but I do need to explain how I can thank the Germans for making this pilgrimage along the Camino possible...twice.

Now you can't just walk into a Catholic Church and say, "We're here, we want to get married!" It's not like Vegas. Not only does the church need to be reserved, but all the paperwork must be in place too. And while the Catholic Church may have as its primary mission of shepherding people closer to God, they have developed quite the bureaucratic labyrinth to usher the flock through.

First of all, the hopeful bride and groom must produce documentation of their baptism, but not just that they were baptized, but an official certificate from the parish church where they were baptized signed within six months prior to the intended date of marriage. If Julie and I had grown up in the same town where we were baptized and if we planned to get married in the same local parish, this might not have been such a difficult feat. But while Julie and I were living in Philadelphia, neither one of us was from there. Julie was born in Yonkers, New York but grew up in Marblehead, Massachusetts. And as I just mentioned, I was born in Hamburg, Germany, but grew up mostly in northern New Jersey, but wasn't confirmed in the Catholic Church until I was in college in Washington, D.C. So, we had to get a Philadelphia priest to authorize certificates from Yonkers and Hamburg, and send all the proper paperwork to a priest in Galicia, Spain.

I'm not sure how easy it would normally be to arrange a wedding in the Cathedral of Santiago de Compostela, but we had an "in." Remember my friend Antonio, the one who presented me with the riddle at the beginning of my pilgrimage? He and I had been working together for over ten years coordinating and chaperoning student exchanges between our two high schools, his just north of Madrid, and mine just north of Philadelphia. He would stay at my house for three weeks while his students were living with families from my school, and then I would stay with him for three weeks while my students were living with families in Spain. After doing these exchanges for a number of years, we had become good friends. When I first told Antonio about Julie, he said he could tell how happy I was. When I called to tell him that Julie and I were getting married, he was very excited.

"You will come to Spain to get married!" he replied in a voice that sounded like a Spanish Louis Armstrong with a three-pack-a-day habit. That's his normal voice. And while he was a smoker, I've learned from meeting his mother, that the gravellyness in his voice is more from genetics than from the cigarettes.

When he said this, I didn't consider it to be anything more than an enthusiastic way of saying congratulations and I am happy for you. "Well, we haven't made any wedding plans yet," I said, "but whenever or wherever it is, you are invited!"

But a couple months later, when Julie and I came up with the wedding-in-Santiago plan, his invitation became a reality. I called him to tell him of our plan, and to our surprise, he told us that he knew the priest of the chapel attached to the Cathedral of Santiago, who was a former professor of his when he studied there. He told us he would ask him about performing the ceremony, and put us in contact to arrange the details. I couldn't believe how this was all working out.

As I mentioned, we figured out the date for the wedding based on how long it would take to walk the Camino and how soon I would be able to start based on when my school year finished. That is how we came up with the date of the eighth of July. So, we contacted Father Juan Filgueires, Antonio's friend, to see if we could book the chapel then. We were in luck. It was available. He told us of all the documents that we would need to send to him ahead of time, and this is where Father Mike, the Philadelphia priest, comes back into the picture.

We needed to have our local parish priest meet with us and sign a number of forms. Fortunately for us, Julie had already gotten her previous marriage annulled, so that wasn't an issue, but we still needed an authorized copy of our baptismal certificates signed within six months of the wedding date. This is where it got tricky. Julie was baptized in a church in Yonkers that no longer existed, apparently closed down or sold or something, and I was baptized in a church in Hamburg, Germany that was in a country I hadn't lived in for over thirty-five years.

Father Mike explained that if a church closed down, they would send all their records to another parish, and he would begin tracking down Julie's document. I, on the other hand, turned to the Internet to see what I could find about mine. I typed in the name of the church that was on my baptismal certificate that my mom had fortunately saved in her filing cabinet all these years, on a search engine, and low and behold, I found a website for the church. It was St. Marien's in Quickborn.

The only glitch was the website was written in German, which is a language I can't read. I tried guessing at some of the words and figured out one of the links was "contact us." That is the nice thing about German. It looks a lot like

English. *"Kontakt"* really isn't that hard to figure out. When I clicked on the link for *Kontaktformular*, a text box came up, which looked like a place to type in a message. Not knowing German, I just typed in a message in English explaining my situation and that I needed a copy of my baptismal record. I then clicked *"Senden."* Seriously, that is apparently how to say "send" in German. I just hoped someone on the other end knew English. Someone did.

I got a response the next day, and within a couple of weeks the document arrived at my house! There is truth to the stereotype of German efficiency. I say stereotype, as I am sure not all Germans are efficient, but I was extremely grateful to the ones working at St. Marien's parish in Quickborn that year. In fact, I got my documents from Germany faster than Julie got hers from Yonkers, but Father Mike was able to track them down, and finally we had cut through all the red tape...or so we thought....

Ironically the term "red tape" has its origins in Spain, and is connected historically to the institution of marriage. "Cutting through the red tape" has come to mean avoiding the often complex and inflexible rules that a bureaucracy creates as obstacles to getting anything done.

It was King Charles V of Spain who started tying important documents with red ribbon to signify they came directly from him and should get priority in processing. The red was a symbol of royalty. Apparently, this practice of using red tape caught on, as King Henry VIII sent his eighty petitions to annul his marriage wrapped in red ribbon to get Pope Clement VII's attention. (Dickson, p. 176).

And while the practice of red tape dates back to the sixteenth century, the modern Catholic Church is still mired in bureaucracy, at least when it comes to trying to get married. So, in addition to the documents validating our baptism, Julie and I also needed a certificate confirming that we had attended the prescribed Pre-Cana course.

What is a Pre-Cana course you ask? The term "Pre-Cana" refers to The New Testament story of when Jesus attends a wedding feast at Cana in Galilee and he performs the miracle of turning water into wine. And, no, the course that Julie and I had to participate in did not teach us how to perform that nifty little trick! The course is designed four couples preparing for marriage to make sure they are prepared for what they are getting themselves into. It's not a bad idea in theory. Seriously, though, what are you going to learn in one afternoon of seminars that might make you rethink the whole "Will you marry me?" question, a question that you were pretty sure you put a lot of thought into already before asking?

One of the sessions was titled "Interfaith Couples." I elbowed Julie and gave her a wink. "We should go to that one!" I said facetiously. Julie was raised Catholic, but no longer went to church, and would probably put herself in the category of recovering-Catholic or no religion at all. In fact, the one sticking point that came up when we were talking about getting married was the fact that I was a practicing Catholic.

With all the hypocrisy that she had seen in the Church, she had pretty much dismissed the religion as a fraud, and wanted nothing to do with it. She told me that her mother once said to her that being a practicing Catholic wasn't the important thing as long as she had a relationship with God. Julie decided that was her out, and was happy not to have religion be part of her life. She decided my faith was acceptable because she called me a "cafeteria Catholic." I took the parts of the religion I liked, and left those that I disagreed with at the counter. I would not exactly describe myself that way, but I had no problem with Julie deciding Catholicism was not for her. That is why I joked about us being an interfaith couple. We didn't end up going to that session.

One session we did attend was called "Sexuality." My first thought was, "What is a priest who has made a vow of celibacy going to know about sex?"

Well, I soon discovered that it was not a priest who was leading that session but rather a married couple from the parish. In fact, the entire course was facilitated by married laypeople. To my surprise, one of those married laypeople was a good friend of mine who taught at the same school where I worked.

When I saw that my friend Michael was going to be part of this, my stress level immediately lowered, as he had a great sense of humor and always had a way of cutting the tension with a joke. I remember attending his wedding not long before when I sat in the pews in the friend section and when he and his new bride recessed down the aisle after making their vows, we all put in these gag "Billy Bob teeth" and smiled at them as they passed. They cracked up. It was pretty funny.

And while my stress level went down, I can't say the same for Julie. She sat through each session that day with her arms crossed and her brow furrowed in what could almost be described as a scowl. She would have been happy to skip the whole thing, but agreed to suffer through it for me.

Anyway, we survived the first few sessions unscathed before moving to the session about sexual relationships in marriage. My friend was not presenting this one, but the couple leading the discussion seemed very nice. You could tell they felt a bit like they had drawn the short straw in having to lead this conversation. Who feels comfortable talking about sex, really? They introduced the topic by telling a story about a trip they took together to the Caribbean and chartered a boat to go scuba diving. I assumed there was supposed to be some metaphor in this little parable they were telling us, but I must admit I wasn't paying attention too closely, because I kept looking over to Julie to see if she was okay. She just sat there slouched in her chair with her arms crossed with a look on her face like she was a school kid who was being made to sit in the corner, being punished for something she hadn't done. I returned my attention to the speakers just at the moment they asked the question,

"Does anyone know the Church's position on sex in a marriage?"

I could see everyone shift in their chairs a bit uncomfortably, avoiding eye contact so as not to be called on. I raised my hand.

"You are supposed to wear scuba gear?" I suggested.

Nobody laughed. Julie left the session with the same notion that she came with, and that was that the Church says you have to "be open to as many children as God gives you." I left scratching my head about two things. I still was not clear about the Church's teaching on sex, and I couldn't believe nobody laughed at my scuba gear joke!

Julie and I survived the Pre Cana course, and she still wanted to marry me. Father Mike now had all the documents that we needed, so the Catholic Church was now ready to marry us. And you now know how the Germans saved the day. Without their efficiency, their expert record keeping, and their ability to read and write in English, I never would have obtained that piece of paper that made the wedding possible. I never met the Germans who helped me, nor did I send them any kind of thank you. I'd like to think that someday I will travel to Germany and visit the place where I was born and maybe get a chance to thank them in person. I did, however, meet some Germans, in person, along the Camino, and they also played a key role in helping me arrive on time for my wedding.

The Essentials

"How's your ass?" asked a stranger with a thick German accent as I approached the reception desk.

This was not a question I was expecting as I entered the hostel in Roncesvalles. To be fair, this was not a question I would expect anywhere, but certainly not there. Standing at the desk waiting to check in, were three German pilgrims, one tall with glasses, one short with a beard, and the other average in every way that he is hard to describe. The rather bizarre question came from the tall one with glasses, but all three were staring at me with a peculiarly pleasant smile waiting for me to respond. I stood there, blank-faced, trying to process this question. "How's your ass?"

My mind was flipping through a Rolodex of possible meanings for this question. Was this a form of greeting in the part of Germany where these three pilgrims were from, and perhaps something was simply lost in translation? Did he mean to say, "How are you?" and because his English wasn't great, it just came out wrong? Was I walking in an odd way that they were conjecturing a reason for it? Was there a stain on my pants that I got from sitting on something by accident? I didn't turn around to look at my butt. I thought about it for a second, but that would have been weird. I could not come to any logical reason for this question, and therefore my response was limited to a simple "fine" and a subtly raised eyebrow to show I did not really understand the question. And that was it for my exchange with these three Germans at this time. They turned back to the receptionist to complete their check-in and proceeded into the hostel where they would settle for the night. When it was my turn to approach the desk, I learned that there were no more beds at this hostel, as they were all reserved, but I could check down the street at the "albergue antiguo" or old hostel.

As dusk was settling on the little village in the mountains, I made my way to the albergue antiguo to find there was plenty of room at the inn, so to speak. This hostel was a large cavernous stone structure that looked like an old church with vaulted arches and a wooden beamed ceiling. And even though it was June, it was cold inside. The giant room was filled with metal bunk beds from end to end which gave this place more the look of a refugee camp than a welcoming hostel. No wonder they are called "*refugios*." I found a free bunk with a mattress that looked in dire need of cleaning and a stain on the stone floor next to it that conjured up the image of a crime scene.

This may have been the worst night of sleep ever in my life. Between the haunting accommodations, the raucous snoring of the endless row of pilgrims, the squeaking of the metal bunks as they tossed and turned, and the penetrating cold of the room, I barely slept a wink. I did not have the advantage of being exhausted from a full day of walking in order to fall asleep. The noise from the early morning rustling of a group of Frenchmen at 5:30am getting ready for the next day's journey was almost a welcome sign of the end to that night's torment. The lights had not even come on yet, so they busied around with headlamps packing up their packs and zipping up their sleeping bags. By 7:00am the overhead lights came on to roust the rest of the pilgrims as everyone had to be out of the albergue by eight, or maybe it was nine. All I know is that I was up and out by 7:15 and already walking my first leg of the Camino. I had three layers of clothes on, as the early morning was very cold coming down out of the mountains.

It was not until three more days of walking that I would discover the meaning to the German's confounding question. If you spend five to seven hours a day walking for three days straight, the friction of the constant back and forth of your legs can cause an extremely uncomfortable rash between your butt cheeks, which makes walking very uncomfortable. So, the question, "How's your ass?" was simply a more efficient way for the Germans to calculate how long other pilgrims had been walking. As I later learned, these three Germans were doctors, so the question was more of an attempt at diagnosis rather than friendly greeting, but it was exactly their ability to diagnose ailments that I would soon owe a debt of gratitude to these Germans once again for making my journey to Santiago possible.

What do you bring with you in your backpack to avoid chafing between your butt cheeks? This was not a question I had thought about, nor did I read about it anywhere in any traveler's guide for preparing for the Camino. I tried to be smart about packing, but the truth was I had no experience in this. Now Julie was the experienced traveler, and I deferred to her to check my backpack before I left. I remember she picked up the pack and immediately said, "You packed too much." She told me the general rule of thumb was not to exceed twenty percent of your own body weight. For me, that meant my pack had to be less than thirty-five pounds. Mine was close to fifty. I had to start the process of shedding stuff so that the only things in my pack were considered essential.

When thinking about packing essentials, I can't help but think of a Brian Regan comedy sketch about losing a bag at the airport. And this was a real fear. What would happen if I arrived in Spain ready to walk the Camino, but my backpack didn't arrive with me? That would be a nightmare. This is probably any airline passenger's nightmare, but even more so, because I wasn't going to be staying in a hotel. I didn't even know where exactly I would be sleeping each night, so I would have nowhere I could tell the airlines to send my bag if and when they did find it. So, the ideal is to pack a backpack that you can check in the overhead compartment so there is no worry about it not arriving with you. But in order to fit in the overhead compartment, my backpack had to have nothing but the essentials. That brings me back to Brian Regan's comedy sketch.

His story begins with him in line at the airport baggage claim office because his luggage never showed up on the carousel when he landed. He is behind all these other irate travelers who are yelling at the agent behind the desk because the airline has lost their bags too. The agent, trying to maintain order, asks the passengers to form three lines. One for angry people, one for livid people, and one for those who want to wring his neck. To placate each complaining traveler whose luggage was lost, the agent promises that the airline will deliver the bags to their hotel rooms. But wait, there is one more thing the agent can do for them! He reaches behind the desk and hands each one a little bag with a zipper on top with a label that says "Essentials Kit." That is when Brian Regan delivers the punchline, "Oh…THESE are the essentials…then I overpacked!"

When Julie told me that I overpacked, I had to decide what was truly essential. I was trying to get my backpack weight down, while at the same time be prepared to have everything I needed for a month of walking. I did not need to think about packing food or shelter, really, as my plan was to stay in *refugios* and eat at local places along the way. Most pilgrims tend to walk the Camino with this plan, and the guidebooks are designed to indicate all the places you can stop along the route to eat or sleep.

I only met one pilgrim along the Camino, a man in his early thirties from France who was walking alone, who brought a tent and a cook stove and food with him while walking. I did see some pilgrims making their own food in some of the hostels, but it was pretty basic stuff, like ramen noodles and such. The French guy seemed to prefer to walk alone and be by himself, so his method of providing his own food and shelter made sense.

But sharing a table with other pilgrims for a meal at a restaurant and bunking with them afterwards at a nearby hostel provided instant community and a natural venue to share stories with people you might otherwise have no cause to meet. I enjoyed these communal opportunities to learn about other people, and I also wanted to experience the local cuisine, and not just survive on ramen noodles. Besides a water bottle and some room for a piece of fruit or a granola bar, I was not planning on packing food or shelter. So, what should you pack?

Well let's start with the backpack. I recommend going to a store that knows how to fit a pack to a person. You really need to try one on to see where it sits on your hips and how it feels on your shoulders. Remember, this thing will be part of you for a month, so you need to make sure it is comfortable. Julie and I went to the local REI store and bought a pair of Mountainsmith Ghost packs, but in two different sizes, as she is smaller than I am. When choosing the size, again you need to think of what is on your list of essentials, and remember the more stuff you bring, the heavier your pack that you are carrying each day...unless of course you choose to have your bag sent from one town to the next, which you can do as there are a number of such services advertised along the Camino. Also, if your backpack does not come with a built-in rain cover, you will definitely want one of those.

Another essential I needed was a pair of hiking boots. I was not a hiker, so I did not already have a pair. Julie had hiking shoes she used on her Nepal trek and her yearlong trip around the world before we met, but I hadn't hiked since I was a kid in boy scouts. I did a lot of research on brands and types, and finally ended up in the local REI store again to try some on. I decided on a pair of Montrail boots that set me back about a hundred and fifty bucks, but I figured if I was going to walk for a month, I better have good boots. Hiking in brand new boots would not be the best idea for starting the Camino as that is just a recipe for blisters, so I decided I needed to break them in a bit, not to mention get in shape for the walk.

As for clothes to pack, I really had to rethink what I was bringing. This is where I needed to pare down to the essentials. I was thinking of all the possible scenarios I might run into and what clothes would be required for each. I was going to be gone a month, but I couldn't pack like I was going on vacation, because my backpack would be way overstuffed and too heavy. I ended up with three t-shirts, two long-sleeve shirts, two pair of zip-off hiking pants, a sweatshirt, a rain jacket, rain pants, four pair of hiking socks, flip flops for the shower, a bathing suit (which I used once in a public pool along the Camino but would need for our honeymoon), a wide-brimmed hat, a toiletry kit, a first aid kit, sun screen, sunglasses, a towel, a sleeping bag, and a walking stick (which has its own story which I will describe more in detail in the next chapter.) The key word for clothes was "wicking!" I had never heard this term before I started to prepare for the Camino, but learned that material that "wicks" away moisture from your body is essential for comfort while walking for long distances with a backpack. Wicking wear also is generally much lighter, which makes for a lighter pack. A flashlight is key, not so much because I would be out walking after dark, but because lights out was pretty strict in most of the hostels, so you would need a flashlight to help you get ready in the morning or find something in the middle of the night. A headlamp is ideal.

I went back and forth about whether or not to bring my iPod. I liked listening to music and I thought it would be nice to listen to music while I walked. But on the other hand, I did not want to program my Camino experience with a soundtrack. If I walked listening to music with earphones, I would effectively be tuning out my surroundings, not to mention discouraging any conversation I might have with fellow pilgrims or listening to "the voice inside your voice, directed to the ear within your ear." These are the words of Buddhist master Beop Jeong, often called the "Thoreau of Korea." And if walking the Camino is to be a spiritual journey, then it is essential to be attentive to that voice inside your voice. With iPods, cell phones, computers, TVs and whatever new technology that comes along, it is very easy to be distracted from hearing your inner voice. Yet I must confess that I spend an inordinate amount of time in my daily life on such devices. I find it difficult to escape this world of technology. Jeong writes about the world we live in as a kind of prison, in which many of us feel trapped.

"The inside of the prison is equipped with refrigerators and washing machines, televisions and stereos. We who live inside here have not the faintest clue that we are trapped within that prison. If you want to escape from this prison of abundance you have to stand and face the most fundamental questions. What is a genuine human being? For what sake are people living? How are we supposed to live? Without facing up to these kinds of questions, you cannot consider such a life to be that of a genuine human. You must always be able to ask, 'Where is my life going?' Who am I?" (Jeong, p.182)

Preparing for this pilgrimage was more than figuring out the essentials to put in my backpack. Yes, I had to attend to my physical needs to make the journey, but what of the spiritual needs? Perhaps this Camino wedding plan was more than just a unique way to elope. Perhaps it was a journey to take some time away from my daily routine to ask the question, "Where is my life going?" Perhaps Julie and I were both looking to give this question the time and space it deserved to be answered. We did not actually share this question with each other out loud, and I don't know if we were even thinking it. I do believe, however, that on some subconscious level, the Camino was calling us to ponder that very question before we arrived in Santiago to exchange vows.

The act of packing my backpack was kind of an oxymoron. I needed to fill my pack with the essentials for my pilgrimage, yet what I was really doing was emptying my life of the non-essentials in order to simplify and focus on the question before me. Was I really ready to get married? To be certain of this answer, the Thoreau of Korea implores us to simplify, and focus on emptying rather than filling up.

> "People usually fill something up completely to the point of overflowing, rather than emptying it. It is only when something is completely empty that the soul's echo can ring inside. We are attached to possessing things and know nothing of emptying. It is only when something is emptied that it can be filled with something new." (Jeong, p.198)

So, there I was, getting ready for the pilgrimage, emptying my backpack so that I could make it lighter. I had to focus on just the essentials. My iPod was not one of them. I decided to leave that behind. One item I packed, not realizing then how useful it would be on my pilgrimage, was my deodorant stick. When I discovered why the German's were asking me "How's your ass?" I needed to find a remedy for chafing of the butt cheeks. Applying the deodorant stick on the left and right buttock where they come in contact with each other does the trick! My ass was good for the rest of the pilgrimage. How come none of the guidebooks mentions this? Applying the deodorant stick to my feet and toes also helped avoid blisters. Make sure to add this to the list of essentials!

The Walking Stick

As I rounded the corner of the trail, there was a clearing with a bearded man sitting at a picnic table with an open box of cookies resting at the edge, a row of walking sticks leaning against the bench, and a sign that said the cookies were free. There is nothing more welcoming to a pilgrim who has been walking for hours than a free snack and a place to sit. As I drew near the table, the bearded man looked at my walking stick and proclaimed, *"¡No es de madera de España!"* Although his greeting seemed a bit abrupt, I had started to get used to rather odd greetings along the Camino.

He was, nevertheless, correct. My walking stick was not made of Spanish wood! At first, I thought this to be a rather random comment to make, but once I considered the source of the comment, it made perfect sense. I learned that the man's name was Marcelino and that he had been a pilgrim himself back in 1977. He was so moved by his experience along the Camino, that when he retired, he decided to devote himself to helping others doing the pilgrimage. He would look for sturdy walking sticks and carve a good handle and point, and offer the sticks for those in need of one along their journey. I had read in my pilgrim's guidebook that a walking stick or bordón was an essential piece of equipment to have for making the trek. It is much more than just the aesthetic "look" of the pilgrim. The bordón is used to help traverse rocky or slippery terrain, keep balance while walking, maintain a rhythm, ward off vagrant dogs, and as I learned first-hand, provide support when the tendonitis in your knees makes going downhill painful. Marcelino had a picture of himself in full pilgrim regalia from back in 1977 displayed on the table, and despite his initial gruff demeanor, he was a kind and generous man who now dedicated himself to helping others. I can only assume he helped Toshi, my fellow pilgrim from Japan, because I recognized the curved branch he had been using when we walked together discarded alongside Marcelino's table. He must have passed by here not long before and opted for a sturdier bordón that Marcelino had crafted. From spending days on end making walking sticks for pilgrims and seeing them come out of the Pyrenees with sticks they had found on their own, it was no wonder he had become an expert in the wood of the pilgrim's staff. I am still amazed, however, that by just looking at the stick, he knew that my stick had not come from any tree native to Spain.

My stick was of yellowish wood with a thin bark. It was about an inch in diameter, and about four and half feet high with a crook about three quarters of the way up right where my hand would rest when my elbow is bent at ninety degrees. I brought this stick with me when I flew from New York to Madrid, and getting it through JFK airport security was an odd story. To be fair, just traveling through the airport dressed in my hiking boots, zip off pants, a backpack clipped around my waist and shoulders, a wide-brimmed canvas hat and holding a wooden walking stick, I felt a bit odd myself. It was much more common to see people wearing a sport coat and a briefcase, or jeans and a baseball cap with a knapsack or computer bag. I felt like the guy who comes to the party dressed as a pirate or a vampire only to realize that when the invitation said, "dress up," it meant to put on a suit and tie and not a costume. But there I was, standing in the security-check line dressed like I was ready to start my trek through the mountains. I was prepared to take off my hiking boots to go through the metal detector, even though I knew it was going to be a pain to unlace them and then lace them up again, but I wasn't thinking that my walking stick would present a problem. I hardly considered it a weapon. But I guess for those that have seen the second Lord of the Rings film, where Gandalf is asked to give up his staff upon entering King Théoden's castle, to which Gandalf pleads to not have an old man be deprived of his walking stick, and then proceeds to incapacitate all of the guards inside with his very powerful wizard's staff, I will concede that perhaps it could be used as a weapon. Maybe my tale has more in common with Frodo's than I thought. Nevertheless, there I was in the airport with an unwelcomed bordón.

The TSA agent at JFK explained to me that I would have to surrender the stick, but as I was preparing to board the plane, they would bring the stick to the gate and allow me to check it as luggage. With all the commotion involved in boarding a plane, I was afraid I would forget to go back and get the stick, but when they announced boarding, I remembered to return to the security check station, and one of the agents walked me to the gate. The agent, of course, carried the stick. I thought that must have looked amusing; a uniformed agent in dress shoes and a tie holding a wooden staff walking next to a hiker with a backpack, and no staff. We got to the gate, where the agent handed me back the stick and said when I got to the end of the jetway I should ask a flight attendant to check it under the plane.

Now, I believed that feigning ignorance is sometimes a more tactful approach than presenting all the information at hand, so when I met the flight attendant, instead of saying I needed to check the stick below the plane, I asked, "What should I do with this?" holding up the stick. She looked at it with a bit of a perplexed expression, and then presented a reasonable solution, "That should fit in the overhead compartment." So, my wooden staff that was to be my companion along the Road to Santiago accompanied me on my flight just above my head. Apparently, it was not such a dangerous weapon after all.

It does beg the question about our perceptions of things. When did a walking stick become a threat? There is no question that since 9/11 we see airline travel as a potential for disaster, and every passenger is eyed with suspicion because of the acts of a few terrorists on that fateful day. The question remains: will we ever be able to return to the times before that day when we didn't view every passenger as a potential threat? Will we have to remove our shoes before boarding a plane from now on? Will we always have our backpacks checked before entering a museum or stadium? Is this just the new normal? I feel as though we could write a few more updated verses to Bob Dylan's "Blowing in the Wind."

> How many times must we take off our shoes
> before we're allowed to board the plane?
> Yes, and how many people will the TSA choose
> before we're all treated the same?
> The answer my friend... may be never again.
> The answer may be never again.

I remember when I lived in Washington, D.C. and was teaching English as a Second Language to adults who had recently immigrated to the country and wanted to learn the language, how proud I was to be an American living in a free society. One day, I decided to take my students on a field trip to the U.S. Capitol Building not only to give them an experience they could write about to practice the language but also to learn a bit about our government. I vividly remember walking from the South Capitol metro station to the steps of the east entrance to the Capitol Building. As I reached the top of the steps, I turned around to find that all of my students had stopped at the bottom. I walked back down the stairs to ask why they had not followed me. They each told me about experiences in their home countries where common citizens were not allowed access to buildings of such importance and they did not think they could enter. Perhaps some were afraid of how they would be treated as non-U.S. citizens. I assured them that they could walk in with me without having anything to fear. This was America, where we are a government of the people, by the people and for the people.

They agreed to follow me up the stairs and as we entered the rotunda, an impressive piece of neo-classical architecture designed to evoke the Pantheon in Rome with statuary and paintings that told of the history of the nation, these ESL students stood in awe. I think the awe was inspired more from the fact that they could freely enter this iconic building that represented such power in the world than from the beauty of the building itself. It was an unforgettable moment for me. Sadly, it may be a moment that I will never be able to replicate, as post 9/11 security measures have turned this freely accessible paragon of democracy into an impenetrable fortress to the common man.

While some argue the measures are necessary to protect democracy and our free society, I wonder if it is now just a symbol of what we have lost. I think of the words of Benjamin Franklin, "Those who would give up essential Liberty, to purchase a little temporary Safety, deserve neither Liberty nor Safety." In any case, I did not lose my walking stick while going through airport security, at least not on this trip. It was also not the first time this walking stick had made a trans-Atlantic voyage.

It was many years earlier that I found this particular staff while climbing Croagh Patrick in the western part of Ireland. It was in 1989, just after graduating college that I traveled to the Emerald Isle with some friends, and, while circum-navigating the island in a rental car staying in B&Bs wherever we ended up, we happened to pass this mountain of legend from the top of which St. Patrick is said to have cast out all the snakes of Ireland. I also heard that St. Patrick went up this mountain and spent forty days and nights in retreat, following the model of Jesus. Apparently during this retreat, snakes attacked him. St. Patrick launched a counter-attack by chasing all the snakes into the sea, and not just the ones attacking him on that mountaintop, but every snake in the country. And from that day forth, there have been no snakes in Ireland.

Scientists would explain the lack of a native snake to Ireland as a result of species migrations after the ice age, and a lack of land bridges and such, but that is not nearly as interesting a tale as St. Patrick the snake-slayer. Whatever the truth is, it had become a pilgrimage site where people would come from all parts of the world to climb this holy mountain. Looking back, it is somewhat ironic that I would find the stick I used to make my pilgrimage to Santiago at the site of another pilgrimage, but at the time, being a pilgrim in Ireland was not my intention. In truth, I don't know what compelled me to climb that mountain that day, but I did. And as I began my ascent, I found a collection of sticks at the base of the trail that others had either left behind or, like Marcelino, had prepared so that others might have the support they needed along their journey. I picked this yellowish one with a slight bend in the staff that seemed to make a perfect grip, and up I went.

My friends had no intention of climbing up the mountain with me that day. It was not because they didn't appreciate the historical, cultural or natural significance of the place. In fact, they might have even been the ones who told me the story of St. Patrick and the snakes, but while they might have been history buffs, they were not fans of physical exertion. If there were a funicular to the top, they would have been first in line to get on, but climbing to the top...not a chance. Climbing Croagh Patrick was never on their itinerary of things to do while in Ireland, we just happened to be driving past it. But when we stopped to take a look at the mountain, and learned about the pilgrimages made to the top and saw so many people choosing to walk to the top, I was intrigued. My friends could tell that there was something calling me to climb up the mountain, so they told me I should do it, and that they would be fine waiting at the bottom until I returned. It took me a few hours to climb to the top and back, so this was truly a sacrifice on their part to just hang out and wait.

The view from the top was breathtaking. The climb to the top and back down was full of adventure and I met some interesting characters along the way. I remember one elderly woman scampering up the trail right past me with the agility of a mountain goat. And there was a couple on their way down, who with their inimitable Irish wit tried to encourage me to keep going by saying the happy hour at the bar on the peak of the mountain was about to close so I had better hurry up. There was no bar. There was, however, this amazing view where you could see the horizon in all directions making it feel like I was on top of the world. I brought my camera, but did not have a panoramic setting on it, so I stood in the same spot, rotating angles and clicking at intervals to capture all three hundred and sixty degrees. I did not have a tripod, but when I got the pictures developed (yes, there was a time before digital photography) the images all connected to form the panoramic view, albeit the edges of the pictures were a bit staggered. I still have the picture hanging in my office. And that walking stick made it on the flight back to the U.S. that summer with no issues, but that was well before 9/11 when airline passengers were just travelers and walking sticks were...well, just pieces of wood.

As I reflect on that trip to Ireland, I think about how my friends and I have grown apart since college. Our careers and life's circumstances took us in different directions. We are still in touch and we see each other from time to time, but we are not close like we once were. Life is not always like a three-hour climb up and down a mountain, where you come back to where you started to find your friends waiting. Sometimes friends take separate paths and you just can't return to a place where you left each other. I was glad they waited that day, especially since we only had one car and getting stranded at the base of some mountain in Ireland would not have been fun. I had kept the stick I found on this pilgrimage up to the top of Croagh Patrick, so when I was preparing for walking the Camino de Santiago, and learned that a walking stick was an essential part of a pilgrim's equipment, I was already prepared with my Irish bordón. I was not prepared, however, to meet a Spaniard with bloodhound-like senses to sniff out non-Spanish wood merely on sight. Marcelino was right.

"No es de madera de España."

The Odd Friar

"*¿Tienes fe?*" I was having a cup of tea and a piece of Spanish tortilla sandwiched in a baguette on the second morning of my journey, when a stocky Spaniard with a full graying beard and ponytail, wearing a gray cassock and a large wooden cross around his neck, donning a baseball cap and hiking boots, turned to me and asked me this question. "Do you have faith?" This was a rather odd question to open with first thing in the morning as you meet a stranger in a café, but there it was. He could easily assume I was walking the pilgrimage due to my backpack with the scallop shell, my hiking boots and my wooden staff, but we had not met before. I took a sip of tea and another bite of my sandwich to give me a moment to contemplate a response.

What did this odd-looking friar in front of me want to know? Perhaps what he was asking was no more than simply taking a survey of what my religious persuasion was, or maybe he wanted to know if I had faith in myself that I would be able to complete the pilgrimage. While I never walked such a distance before in my life, and would not even consider myself a hiker, I did feel pretty confident that I would get to Santiago. Maybe the question was more about the kind of person I was. Was I an optimistic person who believes in the good in himself and in others? I swallowed the bite of tortilla I was chewing, took another sip of tea, and then responded to this inquisitive fellow, *"Sí."* Whatever it was in my rather terse affirmative response, this peculiar pilgrim was prompted to explain to me his reason for walking the Camino.

He introduced himself as Antonio, not to be confused with my friend Antonio who helped me get started on my pilgrimage back in Roncesvalles. I guess Antonio is a common Spanish name. Anyway, this Antonio in the gray cassock lived in a town only a few miles from where we were. He explained that he was separated from his wife and was estranged from his kids, who were now young adults. I gathered from his dress and demeanor that he was atoning for something he had done. My first thought was that he was an alcoholic in recovery, probably because of my own experience with seeing how drinking can hurt a family, but I did not ask. I was there just to listen. While he doubted that he would reconcile with his wife, he regretted not being more a part of his children's lives. He invited his kids to walk the Camino with him in hopes of it being a bonding experience, but none of them was interested. They thought he was foolish and said he wouldn't be able to do it. As I was looking at him while he was talking and thinking he was dressed for a costume party going as Friar Tuck meets John Belushi from Animal House, I could see where his kids might think him foolish. Nevertheless, I admired his motives for walking. Perhaps this odd friar made me think about my relationship with my own father.

My parents divorced when I was eleven years old. My dad moved out of the house and at first, he lived in an apartment down the street, but soon moved to a town over an hour drive away from where I lived with my mom and my older sister. My sister and I would see him a couple of times a month while we were in high school, but by the time we were in college, he had moved to Arizona with his new wife and we would only see each other once, maybe twice, a year. I wasn't resentful of him marrying again. In fact, I was happy that he found someone else to live with, because I worried, for some reason, that he would be lonely living by himself. My eleven-year-old self was often hoping that my parents would be happy, as they so rarely seemed to be when they were together.

I had many memories of my parents' fights, even one where the police were called to break it up. I remember my dad being put into the patrol car in the middle of the night as I watched from my bedroom window. I think I was about four or five at the time. So, when my dad came into my room some seven years later to tell me he and my mom were getting divorced, I should have been expecting it, but I wasn't. It was the late seventies, and divorce was not as common then as it is now. More importantly, they were my parents, and them being together was all I knew, even if they did fight a lot. When my dad left my room after delivering the news, I remember taking a pen from my desk and going to the calendar hanging on my wall and crossing out that day. Not just one X through the box for that day, but so many X's that I tore through the page to the month below. I guess I thought if I could make that day go away, so too would my parents' divorce. But my dad moved that night into a bedroom downstairs, and after a couple of months, into that apartment.

It was in that apartment that I was introduced to the woman who was later to become my dad's third wife. At the time, I thought she was to be his second wife, but in the heat of an argument I was having with my mom sometime later about who knows what, probably taking my dad's side about something, she blurted out, "Yeah, well did you know your father was married before me?" As it turned out, my dad had married and divorced a woman from Germany before he met my mom. They never had kids, and they were not married very long, so I guess there was no reason to have mentioned her. But it did make a pretty dramatic impression on me, especially as it was posed as a question about how much I really knew my dad. Perhaps my dad knew at a young age the importance of having someone walk with you along your journey in life. He just struggled with finding someone compatible.

So, as I was listening to Antonio, the odd-looking pilgrim in the gray cassock, tell his story about his reason for walking the Camino and him trying to reconnect with his college-age kids, I could have been thinking about how I might have responded if my father had invited me to do the same. I think if he had called me when I was in college and invited me to make a pilgrimage together with hopes of bonding, I would have jumped at the opportunity. I would also have been wondering if aliens had possessed my dad's body or if three ghosts had visited him the night before. I am not saying my dad was a Scrooge, but he was never one to talk about his feelings or engage in any deep, philosophical conversations, at least not with me. I remember writing to him about my decision to become a Catholic, and never got a response. Months later, when I flew out to Arizona to visit for Thanksgiving, he turned to me at the dinner table, after the plates had been cleared and we were getting ready for pie, and said, "So, you're a Catholic." I could tell he was trying to wrap his head around this.

My dad grew up in a small town in Maine with a father and stepmother who were Methodists. I don't know about his siblings, but when he left home, he left any religious convictions behind, and for all intents and purposes, was an atheist as long as I knew him. I remember a story my mom would tell of when the local Presbyterian minister asked to come to our house and meet with him after my mom registered the family at the church in town. My mom smiled a knowing smile and said, "Knock yourself out." The minister showed up at the house and sat down with my dad in the living room. In an attempt to find common ground, the minister asked if they could start by agreeing that there is a God and he had a son named Jesus Christ. "You lost me already," replied my dad and then proceeded to ask the minister where his church did its banking. He was a very smart man, my dad, and had a very successful career as a banker, but his focus was on very worldly, practical things.

So, as my dad was trying to understand my very spiritual decision to get confirmed as an adult, he followed up with "I know a couple of colleagues at the bank who are Catholics. It's a good way to network and make business contacts." I had to stop myself from shaking my head in disbelief in how he was processing this. The last thing in my mind when I chose to profess my faith was that it would be a good way to make business contacts! But I could tell that this reasoning would allow my dad to accept the idea of having a Catholic son, so I went with it. "Yeah, I guess so," I said. And that was the end of that conversation.

I don't know if it was my own insecurity or his incommunicative way, but I often thought I disappointed my dad growing up. And when I was graduating from college and asked my dad to come out for the graduation, and when he declined, saying that he had already booked a flight out to the east coast for later in the summer to see some friends and he didn't think it practical to fly out twice in such a short time, I must admit, it hurt deeply at the time. Was this his way of showing his disapproval of my decision to go to college in Washington, D.C. to study international affairs instead of joining the army so that I could get college paid for through the G.I bill like he did? Two years earlier he had not only attended my sister's college graduation, but he bought her a new car as a present. Was this because she saved him tuition money by opting to transfer to a state school? He had set a limit on how much he would pay for college at six thousand dollars a year, which at the time was about half the going rate for tuition for most private universities. I don't know exactly how he arrived at that amount, but I think it had something to do with my mom threatening to take him to court.

I ended up getting an academic scholarship to pay the other half from The American University in Washington, D.C., one of two schools I had applied to. The School of International Studies at American had a good reputation and was in D.C., which was a great place to learn about international relations, the field in which I had hoped to have a career. The only other school I applied to was Georgetown University. I wasn't accepted there. Ironically, Georgetown was a Jesuit school, but it was at American, a school founded by a Methodist bishop, where I became a Catholic. Somewhat ironic, now that I think about it in this context, my dad having Methodist parents and now having a Catholic son.

I was twenty years old when I got confirmed by the university chaplain. My mom, who was raised Catholic, but no longer practiced because of the many church positions on issues that she disagreed with, attended that Easter vigil along with my Uncle Paul who was my godfather from birth. I guess since I was baptized at birth, I could have technically been considered Catholic, but I did not grow up in the faith. When I was in kindergarten, my family moved to New Jersey, where my mom actually made an attempt to get my sister and I enrolled in CCD at the local Catholic church, but when she went to register, she was told she missed the deadline. Despite hearing the explanation that we had just moved, the indignant old nun in charge of religious education told my mom that her only option was to take the books and teach us herself until next year's class enrollment opened up. My mom was not one to take attitude from anyone. She was accustomed to being the one giving it. So, to show this inflexible, bureaucratic, judgmental holy curmudgeon what she could do with her suggestion, she promptly left not only the church but also the entire religion and went shopping for a more welcoming faith community. I think she took her cue from a friend of hers, Montse, a divorcée from Spain who lived in the same town as us in New Jersey, who had a similar experience with the church. My mom tells the story of how her friend Montse brought her kids to the church to register them for classes, but when the priest found out that Montse herself had no intention of becoming a parishioner (for reasons I could only guess at), he would not register her kids. Montse looked the priest in the eye and shook her head saying, "Father, you are a greedy man. I bring you two souls but you will not take them unless you can get three."

It is a shame when people looking to join a community of faith are turned away, but it is more disheartening when those doing the turning away are wearing a habit or a collar. Consequently, after a few months of church shopping, my mother, sister and I ended up at the Presbyterian church downtown that ironically backed up to the parking lot of the Catholic church that shunned us. Now the Presbyterians were not a huge departure from the Catholics, although I guess that depends on your perspective. They were Christian and did the Eucharist too, although instead of a small wafer, they passed around a big loaf of crusty bakery bread and instead of the wine, they passed around little shot glasses of grape juice. When my mom became a deacon in the church, she was in charge of getting the bread and grape juice for Sunday service. I must admit that when we brought the leftovers home and made toast with jelly, some of the mystery was lost. My sister and I went to Sunday school classes and joined the choir, but by the time we got to high school our interest was waning and eventually we just stopped going. So, when I learned of the desire of this odd man in the gray cassock to reconnect with his kids through some kind of spiritual journey, I felt a mix of admiration and envy as I reflected on my younger self.

When he asked me why I was walking the Camino, I responded with the same response I planned to give the hospitalera back in Roncesvalles if she had pressed me for more detail. I was walking to Santiago because I was going to get married there. After walking the first part alone, my fiancée would meet me along the road and we would finish the Camino together and get married there in Santiago. I explained the metaphor of walking alone and walking together representing being single and then being married. Antonio of the Gray Cassock seemed to appreciate my reason for walking as he gave me this approving nod before taking another sip of his coffee. He then turned to Vicente, another pilgrim I met the first day in Roncesvalles, who happened to be in the café that morning too.

Unlike Antonio's pilgrim apparel, Vicente was dressed in bright blue Lycra walking shorts, a tee shirt and sneakers. He was a middle-aged businessman from Valencia who clearly spent most of his workdays sitting at a desk drinking coffee and eating churros. The Lycra walking shorts were not flattering, but were practical, I imagine, if at least for preventing chafing while walking (flashback to the German's question, "How's your ass?") Vicente was on holiday, and as a creature of routine, would walk a week every year on a different part of the Camino, to get some exercise. For Vicente, the Camino de Santiago was like a membership to a health club, which seemed an entirely different motivation than Antonio's. I would meet many more pilgrims along the

Camino and each one with a very unique and personal story. Most conversations with pilgrims you meet along the way start with the question, "So, why are you walking the Camino?"

But Antonio of the Gray Cassock was the only pilgrim I met who opened the conversation with, *"¿Tienes fe?"* I was fortunate that he did not follow up my one-word response with a question asking me to explain what I meant. I don't know what I would have said. And while I did not ask him if he had faith, I guess I could surmise that he did, since, according to Thomas Aquinas, "To one who has faith, no explanation is necessary. To one without faith, no explanation is possible." What was more, neither of us mentioned religion, as if one had nothing to do with the other. I know I just told you about becoming Catholic, but to me, faith and religion are not the same things. I would agree with Richard Rohr who said, "Faith is more how to believe than what to believe." He writes about how faith is more a journey than a destination, and how difficult it is to talk about it.

> "When engaging with one who has not gone through the rings of fire, any attempt to "prove" the existence of God – or even the reasonableness of your own faith – will invariably meet with failure. It can be reasonable only to those who have endured the temporary unknowing darkness, the 'childhood,' and have returned on a different level of awareness…. It makes you feel very powerless or foolish around those who have not made the same journey. It also explains Jesus' frequent, bothersome, and surprising line to his disciples and beneficiaries: 'Don't tell anyone!'… To try to talk about the unsayable to the crowds is to trivialize it, or even to lose its depth…" (Rohr, p. 119)

The three of us finished our breakfast, paid our tabs and

headed out of the café together to continue our walk along the Camino. We each left knowing now why the other was out here walking the Road to Santiago, but I don't think any of us knew exactly where this journey would take us. I don't know where Vicente would leave the Camino to return to Valencia, but he only planned to walk for a few more days. What direction Antonio's journey would take was a little less clear. As for me, I still had my sights set on meeting up with Julie and arriving in Santiago by the eighth of July. And if I came across any other pilgrim who asked me if I had faith, I had my answer. *"Sí."*

The Knights of Malta

The night I spent in Cizur Menor was the strangest night of my journey. As the evening approached, I was trudging uphill on my way out of Pamplona looking for signs for the nearest *refugio* where I might stay the night. Off in the distance, at the top of a hill I saw a flag waving in the wind. At first glance I thought it was a red cross indicating some kind of hospital or first aid station. Perhaps that was what I wanted to see, as my one knee was causing me such pain, I thought I might need medical attention. As I got closer, I realized the colors were reversed and it looked more like the Swiss flag that was flying atop what looked like a small castle. I reached the top of the hill and saw a sign indicating the way to the nearest pilgrim's hostel, which was in the same direction as the small castle with the Swiss flag. As my knees were pleading with me to stop at the nearest *refugio*, I followed the sign that led right to that small castle. The pilgrim's *refugio* WAS the small castle! As I entered, I read a sign explaining that the hostel was run by the Sovereign Order of St. John of Jerusalem, Knights Hospitaller, also known as the Knights of Malta. And the flag flying overhead was the Knight's coat of arms, not the Swiss flag.

I checked in at the front desk, found a lower bunk that was still available to put my stuff on, and began the evening ritual of airing out my boots, doing a quick laundry, washing up, finding a place to eat and then writing in my journal. I took my walking stick with me on my quest to find a place serving a *menú del peregrino* because I really needed it to keep the weight off my knee while walking. On my way back to the hostel, after having found a restaurant just down the street that would serve the pilgrims' meal later on, I noticed a stone chapel just across from the small castle. It had a big wooden door that was slightly ajar so I decided to explore. As I walked in, the temperature dropped about ten degrees. Stone buildings with just a few small windows was the medieval way of installing central air conditioning, which was very welcome in the summer heat of Spain. It was dark inside and empty. It was sparsely furnished, but had a number of portraits hanging on the walls, giving the appearance of more of an art gallery than a chapel. The portraits, I soon realized, were of knights of the order. I have to admit, it was kind of creepy standing alone in this cold, dark, stone room with the eyes of all these dead knights staring at me. After getting a little chill down my spine, I decided to make an exit and head back across the road to the hostel.

There on the steps of the hostel I saw the three Germans I had met on my first day of my pilgrimage. The tall one with glasses introduced himself as Christof, and apparently spoke the best English of the three. He called the short one with the beard Schwenk, and proceeded to tell me why this name was funny, as it had some double meaning, I think, but I didn't really get it, even though I gave a polite chuckle because I realized it was supposed to be funny. And the third German who was nondescript in every way...I don't remember his name. I told them of the restaurant down the street that was serving a pilgrims' meal shortly and invited them to join me. They agreed and we all walked down together. As we ate and talked, I learned that the three of them were doctors on some kind of professional sabbatical, and they decided to spend the time walking the Camino. It was at that dinner that my knee problems were officially diagnosed as patellar tendonitis, which apparently is quite common for pilgrims walking the French Road.

It is a condition caused by excessive stress on the knee and with the weight of the pack and the many downhill roads coming out of the Pyrenees (ha, I just caught that little pun...knees, Pyre-knees!), the knee joints take the brunt of the work. This was not the first time I had been diagnosed with patellar tendonitis. When I was in high school, I was a cross-country runner. I competed on the varsity team for two seasons, and after each season, I ended up in the doctor's office with this same diagnosis. I quit the team after my sophomore year. The truth is I never really enjoyed running. I wanted to play football, but I was undersized and not that good, and my high school football team had a reputation for developing NFL caliber players. In fact, a classmate of mine went on to be a Super Bowl quarterback for the Pittsburgh Steelers. He didn't win that game, but still, pretty impressive. Anyway, all this is to say that I had a history of knee problems.

As the evening meal went on, the wine continued to flow, and the conversations got more lively. The friendly banter jumped from one table to another and soon the whole room was in engaged in one big *tertulia*. Topics of conversation ranged from tips for walking the Camino to family histories to international politics. It was no fun being the American in the group when politics came up, because ultimately someone would ask what I thought about the United States invading Iraq. I had to admit it was not a proud moment for me as an American. I didn't agree with George Bush's policy, and I believe he missed an historic opportunity when the entire world was reaching out to our country in solidarity after the terrorist attack of 9/11. We could have built on this common empathy to strengthen ties between nations and work for peace, but instead we chose to go to war, for what I can only figure was a geopolitical maneuver disguised as revenge. It was disappointing, and it was a topic I tried to pivot from quickly. I saw my opportunity when four women from another table were waving me over.

I don't know if they recognized my predicament and knew I needed saving, or if they were just being social, but whatever the reason, I was happy to join them. I learned that they were nurses from Madrid who all worked together at the same hospital. They were taking vacation together and decided to walk the Camino. I told them of my plans to get married when I arrived in Santiago, not just because most pilgrims ask one another why they are walking, but also to make clear from the get-go that I was not open to a ménage-a-cinq, or whatever you might call that. I told them about the German doctors and their diagnosis of my knee. Rosa, the blond nurse, laughed and said doctors can diagnose, but they don't know how to treat a patient. She turned to Teresa, and pointed to her taped-up ankle, saying that she had twisted it along the road. Then she pointed to Fendi's burned calves and explained the importance of using sunscreen. The fourth one, Ana, who wasn't actually a nurse but worked in the hospital with the other three, had packets of six hundred milligrams of Ibuprofen in her purse and offered them to me.

When we realized we were staying at the same *refugio* that night, Rosa said she could wrap my knee correctly with an ace bandage when we returned. We all returned to the small castle of the Knights of Malta, the four Spanish nurses, the three German doctors and the one hobbled American pilgrim on his way to get married. When Rosa finished wrapping my knee, she recommended that if I were to continue walking, that I should get a pair of *rodilleras* from the local *farmacia* to give my knees extra support. I thanked them for all their help and headed off to my bunk to settle in for the night.

The bunks around me were populated with a various assortment of pilgrims ranging in age, gender, language and nationality, all preparing for bed. Some were coming and going from the bathrooms. Some were repacking their things. Some were lying in bed reading. I got my phone out and texted Julie to see if she could talk. I was six hours ahead, so I knew it wasn't very late back in Philadelphia, but I didn't know if she was free. She was, and so I stepped outside the hostel so I wouldn't disturb anyone and so they wouldn't distract me from listening to Julie's voice. I could sit on the phone for hours with her, just listening, but we had to cut the conversation short as all the pilgrims had to be in the hostel by ten. We said good night and I headed back to my bunk. I wrote in my journal for a bit, and noted that the best part of the night was talking with Julie. "I do love her!!" was the last thing I wrote in that day's entry. Soon the lights went out.

Despite the snoring, the rustling of packs, and the creaking of bunks, I slept pretty well, until I woke in the middle of the night to a glare from a flashlight or headlamp, I couldn't quite make it out, passing through the room. It was almost surreal, like a dream, as the light sort of floated past me in the darkness. I was barely awake and just assumed it was someone finding their way to the bathroom, so I closed my eyes again to go back to sleep. The next thing I knew, I was jolted awake by a blood-curdling scream! I jumped out of bed, and instinctively ran to where I heard the scream come from. I didn't stop to find a flashlight, but didn't need to, as I followed the light from a room down the hall that had been turned on. As I got to the room, I realized it was the room where the four nurses were sleeping, and they were all up and in a panic. I asked them what had happened, and I learned that it was Fendi who had screamed when she saw a strange man standing over her while another one was rifling through her backpack next to her bed. Apparently, the scream and the sound of someone running towards the room caused the two strangers to flee out the door. I looked out towards the exit and then around the hostel, but saw no sign of them. What was even stranger was that the rest of the hostel was quiet. Not one other pilgrim sleeping there seemed to have heard the scream or if they did, decided not to get up and investigate. Rosa went to get her cell phone to call the police. It was four forty-five in the morning. The police showed up just as it started getting light out. We stepped out to give a full report. The police told us that there had been a series of robberies by two *"moros"* who were breaking into pilgrim hostels along this stretch of the Camino. They asked if anything was taken, but apparently, they were scared off before they could take anything.

"You were lucky," they said, "the *hospitalero* of Larrasoaña had taken a serious blow to the head the night before fighting them off when they broke into his *refugio*."

I looked over at the empty desk at the entrance to the hostel and wondered why nobody was watching over this hostel throughout the night. The police asked if there were any other witnesses, and the nurses told them that I was the only one who came running when Fendi screamed. Again, I thought that was strange. I also thought that the use of the term *"moros"* to describe the two robbers was strange. This of course is the Spanish way of saying Moors, which in English seems like a very Shakespearian if not archaic way of describing people.

In Spain, it is rather pejorative. The term "Moor" really doesn't refer to a particular race, religion or ethnicity according to National Geographic. It comes from the Latin "Maurus" which originally described Berbers from the ancient Roman province of Mauretania, which is now North Africa. When North African Muslims captured the Iberian Peninsula and ruled from the year 711 until 1492, they were frequently referred to as the Moors and ruled the land that was then known as Al-Andalus. This land became a prosperous economic and cultural center where the arts and sciences flourished and three major religions; Islam, Judaism and Christianity coexisted peacefully for centuries. Then came the Spanish Reconquista, when the Catholic monarchs fought to reclaim the entire Iberian Peninsula and expelled the Moors, and began the Inquisition, which was not a very proud moment for Catholicism to say the least. But when the police referred to the *"moros"* that had been stealing from pilgrims along the Camino that summer, I doubt the term was intended to conjure up the rich cultural and historic contributions of the Moors in Spain from past centuries. It was more likely a generic, derogatory term to refer to any unidentified dark-skinned foreigner.

The irony of this episode occurring at a hostel that was run by the Knights of Malta was not lost on me. You see, the Knights of Malta were founded first as an order to care for pilgrims traveling to Jerusalem, but as the Holy Land became a battle zone during the Crusades, a series of holy wars instigated by Christians to recover the Holy Land from Islamic rule, the Knights of Malta became a military order that fought to protect Christian pilgrims from attacks by Muslims. This conflict between Christians and Muslims has a long history in Spain, and with a particular connection to St. James. The remains of Santiago, or Saint James, is of course the destination of this particular pilgrimage route, which is the third most popular today among Christians after Rome and Jerusalem. While Saint James is often depicted as a humble pilgrim with a wide brimmed hat and a walking staff, there is another image of Saint James that can be seen throughout Spain that has become quite controversial. This is the image of Santiago Matamoros, or Saint James the Moor-killer. Unlike the image of St. James the pilgrim, Santiago Matamoros sits atop a horse holding a sword high above his head in attack position with a Moorish soldier on the ground below him in a defensive position. The image, according to legend, depicts a scene from the Battle of Clavijo. My guidebook explained that the year was 844 when King Ramiro I of Asturias met the troops of Abderramán II in battle, and in the midst of the fighting, an apparition of St. James the Apostle appeared mounted on a white stallion wielding a sword against the Moorish troops. And while King Ramiro's men were greatly outnumbered, they defeated the Muslims that day, crediting the intercession of the saint.

So, I have a number of issues with this image of Santiago Matamoros. Besides the fact that it reeks of mere medieval propaganda trying to say God is on "our side" and therefore "we" are the good guys and "they" are the bad guys, it is completely contrary to what Jesus actually taught his apostles. In Matthew's Gospel, when one of Jesus' followers drew his sword and attacked one of the men who came to arrest Jesus, he is quoted as saying, "Put your sword back into its sheath, for all who take the sword will perish by the sword." Do you really think Jesus changed his mind about the whole sword thing, and that maybe he should unleash his apostles as swashbuckling warriors in spirit form? I don't think so. But throughout Spain you will see images of Saint James the Moor-killer on a horse with a sword. It is such a sad contradiction to the image of the pilgrim apostle who was charged with spreading Jesus' message of "love your neighbor." There is a movement to remove this iconography, but it is so entrenched in the art and architecture of centuries that I fear this image will remain to muddle the message for generations to come.

You may be thinking at this point that I am making way too much about this word used by the two policemen who arrived that morning at the refugio to describe the thieves that had been stealing from pilgrims. But as I think about the night before at dinner when pilgrims from other countries were asking about America's war in Iraq, I can't help but believe that words matter. In fact, similarly loaded words were used by the President of the United States when explaining his justification of invading Iraq.

> "There could hardly have been a more indelicate gaffe. President Bush vowed on Sunday to "rid the world of evil-doers," then cautioned: "This crusade, this war on terrorism, is going to take a while." Crusade? In strict usage, the word describes the Christian military expeditions a millennium ago to capture the Holy Land from Muslims. But in much of the Islamic world, where history and religion suffuse daily life in ways unfathomable to most Americans, it is shorthand for something else: a cultural and economic Western invasion that, Muslims fear, could subjugate them and desecrate Islam." (Wall Street Journal, September 21, 2001)

These words, "Moors" and "crusade," seem so archaic and yet they are still with us. They are still being used to describe our fellow human beings as "others" and to justify wars by thinking of them as "holy." When will we learn as a human race how to "love your neighbor?"

Martin Luther King, Jr. wrote, "One of the great tragedies of man's long trek along the highway of history has been the limiting of neighborly concern to tribe, race, class, or nation." So why do we put limits on our idea of neighbor? "Who is my neighbor?" This is the question put to Jesus in the Gospel of Luke that leads into his story of the Good

Samaritan. It is a story of a man who, on his way from Jerusalem to Jericho, is beaten and robbed and left for dead along the side of the road. Two people walk by this man without stopping before a third, a Samaritan, with whom the Jews had no dealings in those days, stopped to help. Not only did he tend to his wounds, but he carried him to an inn and paid the innkeeper for his care until he recovered. Jesus explains the term "neighbor" not in terms of shared location, or nationality, or religion. He explains that your neighbor is anyone whom you might encounter that is in need along the road you travel in life.

I found it was easy to be neighborly as I walked along the Camino de Santiago because those walking the road with me were all part of this brotherhood of pilgrims. While we may have been from different countries, spoke different languages, practiced different religions or identified as "different" for any number of reasons, we were all pilgrims sharing this journey towards Santiago. The pilgrimage gave us common purpose that allowed us to see ourselves in others, no matter how different from each other we were. But there, in Cizur Menor, was the first time I faced the reality that the journey could be dangerous. Someone just tried to rob the four nurses. What if, when I got to their room, the two robbers were still there, and what if they had a knife or a gun? The hospitalero in Larrasoaña played the role of the Good Samaritan and protected the pilgrims staying under his roof, but he suffered a blow to the head as a result. It could have been worse. Perhaps the Road to Santiago was not that different than the Road to Jericho. Being neighborly is not just being kind. It also means facing danger.

In Martin Luther King Jr.'s sermon "On Being a Good Neighbor," he points to the Good Samaritan's capacity for what he calls a "dangerous altruism." He did not just do something kind for the man he found along the road. He risked his own life to do it. King asks us to consider why the first two men, the priest and the Levite, did not stop to help the wounded man. What if the robbers were still nearby and attacked them if they stopped to help? What if the wounded man was faking and merely part of some scam to get people to stop so they could be assaulted and robbed? King imagines the first question the priest and the Levite asked was, "If I stop to help this man, what will happen to me?" But what separates the Samaritan from these two is that by choosing to act, he reversed the question. "If I do not stop to help this man, what will happen to him?" This is what King means by "dangerous altruism."

> "The true neighbor will risk his position, his prestige, and even his life for the welfare of others. In dangerous valleys and hazardous pathways, he will lift some bruised and beaten brother to a higher and more noble life." (King, p.26)

I'd like to say that as I left the *refugio* of the Knights of Malta that morning that I was challenged to be a good neighbor, capable of dangerous altruism, but that was not the challenge on my mind. I was, instead, in search of the neighborhood farmacia where I could buy a pair of rodilleras to help me face my own challenge of continuing my journey along the Camino. I found one just down the street, but it did not open until nine. It was barely eight, as my morning had gotten off to an early start due to all the excitement of the Moorish invasion of the castle of the Knights of Malta. I decided I would wait. I took off my backpack, leaned it up against the storefront window and sat down on the sidewalk in front of the entrance to the *farmacia*. I got out my journal and began to write.

It was here that I first thought about writing a book about my journey along the Camino, my journey to meet Julie and get married. At least that was what I wrote in my journal. I started keeping a record of all the people I had met. I wrote down the name of the *hospitalero* from Larrasoaña, Santiago Zubiri, because he was the true knight who protected the pilgrims, the one who embodied "dangerous altruism." And as I sat writing about the irony of the absence of any protectors at the hostel run by the "Knights of Malta," I watched as pilgrims passed by me as they started their day's journey to the next town. Many of them I recognized from the night before. I wondered if I might not see them again, as they were getting an early start, and I would not be leaving for at least another hour. I wrote about this pressure to keep up with the current of the Camino, or at least stay on track to make it to León in time, where I planned to meet up with Julie.

I thought for a second about not waiting around and just finding a pharmacy further down the Camino to get the knee braces so I could make better time, but as I saw the four nurses making their way past me, I decided I had best heed their advice, especially since they just saw me waiting there to get a pair of knee braces as instructed. I gave them a wave and a smile and they continued on. Then I saw the three Germans walk by. I waved and shouted the customary *"Buen Camino!"* Others passed me by as the flow of pilgrims picked up. I wondered if I would see the now infamous "two Moors" pass by, and even if I did, how would I know, considering I never laid eyes on them in the first place. I continued writing, listing all I could remember about the many pilgrims I had met already along the road, until finally, a young woman in a white coat, holding a set of keys in her hand approached and unlocked the door to the *farmacia*.

The Orange

As I continued west along the Camino de Santiago the landscape of Spain changed from steep mountain trails, lush green hillsides and vineyards to yellow fields, dry trails and an expanding horizon that let you see the next town from miles away. It is a bit of a tease, really, as you can see the next town right there nestled in a valley, and yet it is still hours of walking before you get there. There is no question that the sun is hotter here too, and the chances of finding shade are fewer. Today's walk was all sun, and I made sure to put on the sunscreen and was thankful for the wide-brimmed hat that kept the sun off my ears and the back of my neck. Despite the more barren countryside, this part of the trek had its little surprises.

While walking for what seemed over an hour in the direct sun and no trees for shade, suddenly I came upon this stone shelter. It was just there alongside the road. It looked like it had stood there for centuries, built of old stone, like those used for the many churches along the way of St. James. It was an A-framed structure about twenty feet high at its peak. Two Romanesque arches about ten feet high stood side-by-side inviting passersby to enter. The temperature dropped about ten degrees as you stepped in to the tiny roadside temple that was enclosed by stone walls on all sides except the entrance, and steps that led downward towards a basin of water. Was this an ancient bathhouse? A fancy trough from which the local cows could drink? There was no sign explaining its purpose or telling visitors to keep out, so I entered and took advantage of a cool place to take a rest. I wondered if the water was safe to drink, but decided it best to let it sit. Anyway, I still had water left in my canteen. I wondered how long this structure had been there and how many pilgrims would have stopped here for this very purpose, to get out of the sun for a while and rest. Whatever the purpose of this building, it was a welcomed stop along this route. I put down my pack and got out my journal and wrote for a while.

Not a single pilgrim came along while I was sitting there on the steps writing, or at least none that I noticed. Sometimes I can get in the zone and not be very aware of my surroundings. But then I wondered if the reason I had not seen any other pilgrims is that maybe I was not on the right road. My heart started beating a bit faster. I had started walking that day with Vicente from Valencia, a kind of fun alliteration that I swear I did not make up, but we arrived at a spot where he said he knew of a shortcut that veered off from the marked path. He invited me to join him but I declined. It's not that I didn't enjoy his company, but he was walking at a pace a bit faster than me, (no doubt those blue spandex shorts of his were more aerodynamic than my zip-off-below-the-knee hiking pants) so I did not know how long I could keep up with him. And since this shortcut was not on my map, and not marked by any yellow arrows, what would happen if I lost him? No, I decided to err on the side of safety and stay on the main road marked by the arrows. As Vicente of Valencia veered off the verified route through the verdant valley on his variant voyage, I vacillated. (Sorry, I couldn't help myself. V for Vendetta is one of my favorite movies, and I couldn't pass up the chance to venerate it!) I wondered how he first found that alternate route. He had walked the Camino for many years, a week at a time, so I believed he did find a shortcut, but how did he first discover it? Was he walking with some other pilgrim who showed it to him? And what is the point of a shortcut on the Camino? I guess if you have already seen this stretch of road and were not interested in seeing it again, or if you were feeling tired or sore and wanted to shorten the distance to the next refugio, or maybe there was something along this other route that was calling him. I don't know the answer because I did not follow him. But as I sat in the shade of this old stone temple writing in my journal, not seeing another soul pass by, I wondered if perhaps the shortcut that Vicente took had become the main choice for pilgrims, and I was somehow out of step with everyone. I also wondered if perhaps in walking alone, I had missed an arrow along the way and veered off in the wrong direction. It was this moment of panic of possibly being lost that motivated me to put my journal away, take a swig of water from my canteen, strap on my backpack and head out into the sun and continue along the Camino.

My pace picked up a bit as I anxiously looked for the next yellow arrow to assure me that I was indeed on the right road. I felt like I must have walked for miles before I saw an arrow. Finally, painted on a large reddish-brown crag of a rock formation lining the road, was the elusive yellow mark I was searching for. I was indeed still on the right path. But there was still no sign of the next town and my canteen was getting low. I also did not have any granola bars left in my pack, and I was starting to get hungry.

As the late afternoon sun was beating down on me, all I could think of was my dry mouth and empty stomach. Maybe I should have bought some extra water bottles at a bar I passed and put them in my bag, but then I would have more weight to carry. Would it have been worth putting a box of granola bars in my pack, but that too would have been more weight and then I would have the box, wrappers and empty plastic bottles to carry with me until I found a proper place to dispose of them. That could also be for miles. Why couldn't someone invent something you could carry with you, something that came in a biodegradable container so you could leave it on the ground, something that could sate your hunger and quench your thirst at the same time? And perhaps it could come in an easy packable container so the hard corners of a box wouldn't protrude through the nylon of your backpack causing it to rip.

The road before me started an uphill climb and I could not get my mind off finding some food and drink. And then, like a mirage in the desert, there appeared a lone tree alongside the road up in the distance. As I got closer, I saw there were people sitting in the shade of the tree. It was the four nurses I had met back in Cizur Menor! One of them, Fendi, invited me over, and extending her arm, offered me an orange. They were peeling oranges there in the shade of this lone tree and tossing the peels on the ground. An orange. Of course! This was exactly what I was hoping for...something to quench my thirst and sate my hunger at the same time. And it is totally biodegradable so I didn't have to worry about carrying any trash with me after I consumed it. It was delicious. It was the best orange I ever had. Finding the four nurses there in this oasis-like shade of the tree, offering me the exact thing I was craving along my lone, desolate journey, I couldn't help but feel like I was in some episode of the Odyssey where a chance encounter with mythical beings was intended to teach me some moral lesson. I thanked my four fellow pilgrims for their hospitality and headed back up the road to continue my journey that day, and as I walked, I pondered the lesson of the orange.

Why, when I was worried about eating or drinking, was I thinking about what to buy and if there was a product invented by someone that would meet my needs at that moment. Here I was, a pilgrim out on the road hoping to leave the materialistic world behind, if for only a while, and yet, when faced with a need, my first thought was what product could I buy. When I couldn't think of what to buy, my mind immediately went to the need for someone to invent something. But something already had been invented. The orange.

"Oh you of little faith...do not worry and say 'What are we to eat?' or 'What are we to drink?' Your heavenly Father knows that you need them all."

These words from the Gospel of Matthew spoke to me. Now don't get me wrong. I wasn't thinking that I could stop worrying about eating and drinking, because God was going to continually drop oranges from heaven whenever I needed them. But the unexpected orange being offered to me did make me think about how I think. My first thoughts are usually very materialistic. They are about my needs. And at that time my needs were about finding something to eat and drink. And when looking for the answer, my first thoughts were very consumer-oriented. Where can I buy what I need? Surely all my needs can be met by something I can find in a store.

"But seek first the kingdom of God and his righteousness, and all these things will be given you besides."

This is what Jesus' message goes on to say. Not that you shouldn't think about your basic needs, but don't lose sight of your spiritual needs. And isn't the reason for going on a pilgrimage often about some spiritual journey? If I was really just worried about eating and drinking, I could have stayed at home, where I know exactly where the supermarket is, and I have a well laid out routine that allows me to work to earn money to pay for the groceries so that I can eat and drink, so that I can have the energy to work and to earn money and go to the supermarket and pay for groceries so that I can eat and drink...ok, you get the picture. It is a vicious cycle, but a very basic human one, especially for someone who lives in a capitalist economy like I do. But what else is there to life? Some might say nothing. An orange is just an orange. It is just part of nature. And besides, while we didn't necessarily invent oranges, we can certainly take a seed from an orange and plant trees that will grow more. We can then carefully cultivate orange groves and have as many oranges as we need. We can even freeze oranges for later because we invented refrigeration, and we can flavor things like oranges by extracting...well, honestly, I don't know how we do that, but I know we do. I'm getting ahead of myself, though. Let's go back to the part where we take a seed from an orange. Don't we need an orange first before we take a seed from it to plant more? So, which comes first, the orange or the seed?

You probably see where I am going with this. It is the age-old riddle that has sparked debate over which came first, the chicken or the egg? And all too often this debate forces us into one of two camps, the scientific or the religious...the scientific camp looking to empirical evidence and principles of evolutionary biology while the religious camp looking at dogma, tradition or faith. Some in the religious camp would say God created chickens, it says so in the Bible...on the fifth day...God created "all kinds of winged birds." Boom, there it is, end of story, riddle solved. Then there are those in the scientific camp who would point to archaeological evidence that suggests the first red junglefowl was domesticated some ten thousand years ago, but with DNA evidence and mathematical simulations, the domestic chicken may have evolved from a species of birds some tens of thousands of years earlier. But, evidence for amniotic eggs shows they existed some three-hundred and forty million years ago, so perhaps the answer is the egg, but clearly not on the fifth day. Neither argument is my own. The first comes from the book of Genesis in the Bible, which I mentioned, and the second comes from the website of the Australian Academy of Science. Once again, though, I find this to be a false dilemma. I don't think you have to choose between science and religion. The goal of both is to seek answers to life's questions. In fact, I think seeking one without thinking of the other leads to folly.

Galileo was written off as heretic and a madman because he introduced a new way of understanding how the world worked. It was easier to dismiss him because the alternative would be to admit one's own ignorance and have to accept the task of studying science to fully understand what he was saying. But scientists should not get too smug about their advanced thinking when they write off Christians as foolish people who believe in an old guy with a white beard who lives in the clouds and controls everything down here on earth. Understanding Christianity, or some other religion for that matter, is not something simple to grasp. As C.S. Lewis writes,

"...if you want to go on and ask what is really happening – then you must be prepared for something difficult."

He contends that many of the people who object to religion, or Christianity in particular "put up a version of Christianity suitable for a child of six and make that the object of their attack" without accepting that fully grasping an understanding of God is a much more complicated and difficult task.

"Reality," Lewis explains, "is usually something you could not have guessed. That is one of the reasons I believe Christianity. It is a religion you could not have guessed. If it offered us just the kind of universe we had always expected, I should feel we were making it up. But, in fact, it is not the sort of thing anyone would have made up. It has just that queer twist about it that real things have." (Lewis, p.43)

When I was a student in high school, I was not a strong math student, but I loved Geometry. I think it was the proofs, and the logic behind them. Perhaps that is why I am partial to Thomas Aquinas and his five proofs of God. In his first proof, he acknowledges the world is in a constant state of change, which would not contradict Darwin's theory of evolution, but argues that whatever is changing is caused to change by something else. Much like the chicken and the egg, this sets up an infinitely long chain of causation and change that must begin somewhere. There must be something that causes change that is not a result of change itself. This "unmoved mover" is God.

For the scientific community, one theory for the starting point of evolution is the Big Bang. In 1927, a Belgian astronomer, mathematician and physicist named Georges Lemaître proposed a theory of an expanding model for the universe that was later confirmed by Edwin Hubble. Lemaître later hypothesized that the universe started with the explosion of some "primeval atom," which becomes known as the Big Bang Theory (also the name of a really funny sitcom!) There is an irony to this story that flies in the face of a conflict between science and religion. George Lemaître was also a Catholic priest. In fact, there are many famous scientists with deep religious convictions. Gregor Mendel, founder of the science of genetics, was an Augustinian friar. Blaise Pascal, in addition to being a famous mathematician and physicist, was also a Catholic theologian. French astronomer Jean-Félix Picard, who is credited with being the first person to accurately measure the Earth, was a Jesuit. (I wonder if he inspired the name of the captain in Star Trek:

The Next Generation...another great show!) I guess my point is you don't have to pick one or the other. Scientists can explore their faith, and people of faith can explore science. You can do both.

Martin Luther King, Jr. wrote about the widespread belief that there is a conflict between science and religion. "But this is not true," he states.

> "There may be a conflict between soft-minded religionists and tough-minded scientists, but not between science and religion. Their respective worlds are different and their methods are dissimilar. Science investigates; religion interprets. Science gives man knowledge that is power; religion gives man wisdom that is control. Science deals mainly with facts; religion deals mainly with values. The two are not rivals. They are complementary. Science keeps religion from sinking into the valley of crippling irrationalism and paralyzing obscurantism. Religion prevents science from falling into the marsh of obsolete materialism and moral nihilism." (King, p.4)

Dr. King writes about the importance of cultivating a "tough mind and a tender heart." He points out that the dangers of "soft mindedness" can lead to a world where dictators can rule. He cites Hitler's words in *Mein Kampf* when he said, "I use emotion for the many and reserve reason for the few." He then points to politicians in his own country and in his own times who take advantage of soft mindedness of their constituents "with insidious zeal" and who "make inflammatory statements and disseminate distortions and half-truths that arouse abnormal fears and morbid antipathies...leaving them so confused that they are led to acts of meanness and violence that no normal person commits." (King, p.5) Perhaps one of the reasons I chose to become a teacher is to help cultivate tough-minded thinkers that can use reason and intellect so that young people will grow into informed citizens who can recognize when they are being duped by leaders who play on emotions and ignorance. But Dr. King warns us that we must not stop with the cultivation of a tough mind.

"Tough mindedness without tenderheartedness is cold and detached, leaving one's life in a perpetual winter devoid of the warmth of spring and the gentle heat of summer." (King, p.5)

Maybe that is why I chose to make this pilgrimage and get married to Julie...to cultivate a tender heart and be open to love. Speaking of the "gentle heat of summer," that afternoon sun along this part of the Camino seemed to get hotter as the day wore on, and I needed to find the next refugio and call it a day. All this exposure to the sun may have been getting to me with all these philosophical musings about God and oranges. For the record, I am neither a scientist nor a theologian. I am merely a high school Spanish teacher who fell in love with a woman and was walking this pilgrimage route on the way to marry her. If you asked me to probe much deeper into the theories and ideas of any of the people I quoted above, I fear I would greatly disappoint in my answers. I am still trying to work out these questions for myself. It is all part of the journey, I guess. Let me just wrap this up by saying, when I was given that orange by the four nurses along the road, it made me think about God. It also inspired me to buy two more oranges at a market when I arrived in the next town. Spain sure grows some tasty oranges.

The Canadian Smoker

She would have been about my age, medium bob haircut, blonde, in good shape, clearly an outdoorsy type from the complexion of her skin. Maybe she just got the tan from being on the Camino for enough sunny days, but a week on the road did not have the same impact on my skin, or my level of fitness. Yet contrary to what would otherwise be a picture of health, she was sitting on a stone wall indulging a cigarette. By the way she talked, you could tell she was from Canada, the pronunciation of the letter "o" and the frequent "eh", and by the things she said you could tell she was bitter about something. She said it was the need to quit smoking that brought her out to walk the Camino, and she said it was that, which was making her bitter. I don't remember her name, so I just refer to her as the Canadian Smoker. It's funny how you can remember people but you don't always remember their names, so you make up a moniker for them, usually having to do with their appearance, or what they do, or how they interacted with you. So, this woman was simply "the Canadian Smoker."

I am always impressed when others remember my name and call me by it when they see me. Too often I will run into someone that I know, but their name will escape me and I will be embarrassed to the point where I will try to avoid them just so I won't have to admit I forget their name. It's a shame, really, because I enjoy talking with other people, but not remembering a name will force me to become awkwardly antisocial. In the case of the Canadian Smoker, though, there is nothing embarrassing about forgetting her name, because in reality I never met her. In fact, she is not even a real person. She is a character from the movie "The Way" directed by Emilio Estevez and starring his father, Martin Sheen. I saw this movie years after I walked the Camino myself, and I have to admit that it did an excellent job capturing the essence of the experience of this modern-day pilgrimage. There were so many moments during the film that reminded me of things that happened to me or of people that I met along the way. I don't know if every pilgrim to walk the Camino de Santiago would agree, but for me this movie was wonderfully nostalgic and authentic. I can easily imagine that this Canadian Smoker was based on a real person walking the Camino.

While it would not be difficult to look up the character's name on some website that lists cast members of films, her name was not the important thing. It was what the smoker from Canada was going through, and her story that made an impression on me. From the time we meet her, she is verbally lashing out, especially at the protagonist of the film whom she calls "Boomer," played by Martin Sheen. It is not until she physically lashes out at him that we learn her back-story and why she is so angry and what she is doing walking the Camino de Santiago all by herself. As Boomer is packing up to head out on the day's leg of the journey, he drops the box carrying the ashes of his son, which, by the way, is the reason he is walking the Camino. The Canadian Smoker reaches to get it, not knowing its contents, but Boomer grabs her arm to stop her. She instinctively reacts by turning and hitting him in the head to make him back off. The two of them stand there apart, dazed, not knowing what to make of the unexpected altercation. She steps back and utters in a half sob, "I'm sorry." No other words are exchanged.

The next scene picks up later in the day with Boomer walking by himself, ahead of the others. The Canadian Smoker catches up to him looking for a chance to explain. We learn that she was married and pregnant, but in an abusive relationship. Instead of bringing an innocent child into the world to be beaten by her father, she decides to terminate the pregnancy. She tells Boomer that even though the child was never born, she can sometimes hear her voice, imagining what it would have sounded like. Boomer stops and gives her a compassionate look that by itself should have earned Martin Sheen an Oscar, and says, "I'm sorry about your baby," to which she responds, "I'm sorry about yours." This is one of the most powerful scenes in the movie when these two characters share the pain of the loss of their children. It is the point in the movie where these two antagonistic personalities start to treat each other with compassion.

Why is it that people have trouble showing compassion to others unless they know their back-story? Why do we tend to want to judge others rather than show kindness and mercy? This is especially puzzling when we know people are suffering or in pain. We never meet the abusive husband the Canadian smoker mentions in the movie. He is an abstract character, faceless, and yet plays a key role in the plot and the character development of one of the four main pilgrims in "The Way." This faceless, nameless character reminds me of a homily I recently heard given by my local parish priest, Father Fleming.

The gospel reading was from John 8:1-12 where the scribes and Pharisees bring a woman caught in adultery to Jesus saying that she should be stoned to death according the law of Moses. According to the gospel, they are trying to test Jesus to have some charge to bring against him. It is quite a diabolical trap. If he suggests that they not stone her, then he is contradicting the law, and thus they would have grounds to arrest him. But if he agrees to have her stoned, then he would be contradicting his own teachings on love and mercy and forgiveness and perhaps lose his standing with his followers. Given these two choices, it appears there is no good solution. Jesus does not respond at first but instead bends down and writes on the ground with his finger. When they continue to push him for an answer, he utters those oft-quoted words,

"Let the one among you who is without sin be the first to throw a stone at her."

Then he bends down to write on the ground again. One by one, the crowd of scribes and Pharisees disperse until no one is left but the woman and Jesus.

"Where are they?" Jesus asks her. "Has no one condemned you?"

She replies, "No one, sir."

"Neither do I condemn you," says Jesus, "Go, and from now on do not sin anymore."

Father Fleming started his homily saying that if, God willing, he ever gets to heaven, there are two questions he would like to ask Jesus about this particular passage. The first is "Where is the man in this story?" The second question is "What was Jesus writing on the ground?" One reason I usually like listening to Fr. Fleming's homilies is that he often challenges me to think about things from a different perspective. What was the back-story of the man and woman who committed adultery and why wasn't the man mentioned in this story? What sins had the Pharisees committed that they were thinking about as they walked away without casting a stone? I imagine each of them had an interesting back-story as well that explained what brought them to Jesus that day with a stone in their hand. Father

Fleming never conjectures about what Jesus might have been writing, but his question certainly got me to thinking.

I thought about the women in my life that may have found themselves in a similar predicament to the Canadian Smoker, for I am quite sure I know them, even if I have not heard their stories. They are our mothers, our sisters, our daughters, our wives, and our friends. Each has their own story, even if many have never shared it, because it would be too painful. If we knew their stories, I think we would be less likely to judge and more likely to show compassion. And why. as a society today, are we still standing in front of these women with stones in our hands?

The political debate about abortion in our country, and in most places in the world, is based on an antagonistic premise of either this or that. You are either Pro-Life or Pro-Choice. There are only two options. One of them is right and one of them is wrong. And since we have no luck convincing the other side, we show up with stones in our hands. Some believe that the debate will finally be resolved by a decision in the Supreme Court. Others believe it will be settled by passing a law in Congress. But history shows that neither of these actions will bring these two sides together, and so we are stuck in this endless battle between those who view themselves as protectors of innocent lives and those who view themselves as protectors of women's rights. As long as we continue to frame this debate as "either/or" we will never be able to move forward.

If I may conjecture, maybe the words Jesus was writing on the ground were "both/and." Maybe the scribes and Pharisees were BOTH right about the woman committing a sin AND wrong to want to stone her to death for her act of adultery. Maybe the woman was BOTH right to expect mercy and compassion and not be alone standing in judgment AND wrong for engaging in adultery in the first place. In the gospel passage, Jesus does not take sides. He does not say to the Pharisees, "You are just in your accusations and therefore should stone this woman to death." Nor does he tell the woman that committing adultery is okay. He BOTH reminds the Pharisees to be careful about judging others without thinking about how their own sins might be judged AND tells the woman to stop sinning. What do you think Jesus would say if he were standing between two groups of people protesting on the steps of the Supreme Court, each holding up their respective signs for Pro-Life and Pro-Choice yelling at one another?

People may ask me where I stand on the issue as a Catholic. Isn't the Church's position on abortion clear? According to the Vatican Charter on the Rights of the Family, "Human life must be respected and protected absolutely from the moment of conception. Abortion is a direct violation of the fundamental right to life of the human being." Shouldn't I be standing with the Pro-Life crowd? But according to *Gaudium et Spes* in the Pastoral Constitution on the Church in the Modern World from Vatican II, freedom of choice is at the core of the relationship between people and God. In Chapter 1 on The Dignity of the Human Person it is written, "For God has willed that man remain under the control of his own decisions, so that he can seek his Creator spontaneously, and come freely to utter and blissful perfection through loyalty to Him. Hence man's dignity demands that he act according to a knowing and free choice that is personally motivated and prompted from within, not under blind internal impulse nor by mere external pressure." Shouldn't I be standing with the Pro-Choice crowd? Apparently which side to take is not so clear, even for a Catholic! Perhaps the problem is that we are framing this issue as a false dilemma, one of either/or and not both/and. Richard Rohr, a Franciscan Friar and spiritual writer, explains, "...the human mind prefers to think by comparison and differentiation-from. It starts as a binary system, something like a computer." He suggests that we need to reframe false dilemmas if we are to get beyond the conflicts that dualistic thinking creates.

"Polarity thinking is unfortunately a self-canceling system, a form of argumentation that merely lets both sides more deeply invest in and identify with their position. Words can always be fashioned to make our point, and even we know that it is not necessarily objectively or totally true. Ask any lawyer or judge, or honest husband and wife, if that is not the case. If truth is so obvious, why would we need a Supreme Court to resolve disputes? And even the justices disagree with one another, often vociferously! Thus, most groups divide into liberals and conservatives of some sort, thinking that by defeating the other, they will win. This appeals to our competitive nature. The truth, however, is always something other than what one side says about the other. The creating of false alternatives to force a person into an either-or choice, which can occur even with well-intentioned people, is even more characteristic of hostile or insincere opponents, as we see the enemies of Jesus exemplify.... Polarity thinking avoids all subtlety and discrimination and creates false dichotomies. If you fight dualistic thinkers directly, you are forced to become dualistic yourself. This is why, classically, Jesus sidesteps the two alternatives by telling a story, keeping silent, or sometimes presenting a third alternative that utterly reframes the false dilemma. Rhetorically, Jesus was really a genius." (Rohr, p. 99-100)

So, if you ask me where I stand on the issue of abortion as a Catholic...am I either Pro-Life or Pro-Choice?... I would ask you to reframe this false dilemma. I am both Pro-Life and Pro-Choice. I believe in the sanctity of life and I think we as a society need to do better about avoiding unwanted pregnancies. I think we are too cavalier about sex. I think people all too often engage in sexual relationships for the wrong reasons and ignore the emotional and spiritual impact that such intimacy can have. Yes, we are biological beings with physical needs, but we are also spiritual beings searching for what it means to love, and by extension what it means to make love. I also believe that God created us to exercise our free will, because "free will, though it makes evil possible, is also the only thing that makes possible any love or goodness or joy worth having.... The happiness which God designs for His higher creatures is the happiness of being freely, voluntarily united to Him and to each other in an ecstasy of love and delight compared with which the most rapturous love between [two people] on this earth is mere milk and water. And for that they must be free." (Lewis, p.48)

And this is why I found the character of the Canadian Smoker so compelling. She was wrestling with the complexities of her emotions about the loss of her baby and she was not portrayed as either hero or villain, but simply human. She made the choice to end her pregnancy and she understood the reason for her decision. She also deeply felt the pain of this loss and was struggling with how to move on with her life. Maybe that is when she took up smoking. Maybe that is why she found herself walking the Camino de Santiago. All we know is that she shares her story with Boomer to explain why she so violently reacted to him that morning when he grabbed her arm, and in so doing, finds compassion from a stranger she meets along the road. Boomer does not condemn her for having an abortion, nor does he congratulate her for exercising her right to choose. He simply responds with empathy saying, "I'm sorry about your baby." When the Canadian Smoker reaches the end of the Camino, and she stands with her fellow pilgrims on the shore of the Atlantic, with waves crashing against the rocks, she realizes she has come to the end of her journey. She takes out her pack of cigarettes, but instead of throwing them to the sea, she puts another to her lips and lights it. She exchanges a wry grin with her newfound friends and says, "This was never about quitting these things...but you knew that."

So, while the Canadian Smoker is only a fictional character, I imagine there were pilgrims I passed along the Camino who were wrestling with similar issues. I am sure I know women whom I passed in my life's journey who experienced what the Canadian Smoker did, yet they did not share their stories with me. I understand why. If they had, I would like to think I would have responded with empathy and love to help them carry their burden as they continued walking their own paths.

The Poem on the Wall

On the road from Navarette to Najera I stopped at a wall. The wall was an eight-foot concrete barrier separating the road on which I was walking from the neighborhood behind it. There was nothing picturesque about this wall, nor was there much to look at in this neighborhood. I stopped because there was a poem written there, with black paint in a rather informal calligraphy, yet even and artistic, taking up seven panels of the wall. This is what was written:

> Polvo, barro, sol y lluvia
> es Camino de Santiago.
> Millares de peregrinos
> y más de un millar de años.
>
> Peregrino, ¿Quién te llama?
> ¿Qué fuerza oculta te atrae?
> Ni el Campo de las Estrellas
> ni las grandes catedrales.
>
> No es la bravura navarra,
> ni el vino de los riojanos
> ni los mariscos gallegos
> ni los campos castellanos.

Peregrino, ¿Quién te llama?
¿Qué fuerza oculta te atrae?
Ni las gentes del Camino
ni las costumbres rurales.

No es la historia y la cultura,
ni el gallo de la Calzada
ni el palacio de Gaudí
ni el Castillo Ponferrada.

Todo lo veo al pasar,
y es un gozo verlo todo,
mas la voz que a mi me llama
la siento mucho más hondo.

La fuerza que a mi me empuja
la fuerza que a mi me atrae,
no sé explicarla ni yo
¡Sólo el de Arriba lo sabe!

Before those of you who don't read Spanish start complaining, I promise I will translate it. But before I do, let me explain the challenges of translating poetry. Unlike prose, poetry has rhyme and meter and imagery and other literary devices that add to the artistry of the message and give the poem its beauty. A simple word-for-word translation would not do any poem justice, and so the translator is often caught in the dilemma of staying true to the meaning or staying true to the form. I am going to do my best to translate this poem and capture the meaning, and therefore I may lose the rhyme and the meter and probably a lot more. To be able to translate poetry well, I think the translator needs to be a poet themself. I am no poet. Here goes:

> The Camino de Santiago
> is dust, sun, mud and rain.
> Thousands of pilgrims will walk it
> for a thousand years now and again.
>
> Pilgrim, who is calling you?
> What hidden force at you pulls?
> It is not the Field of Stars
> nor is it the great cathedrals.
>
> It is not the Navarrese bravado,
> nor the wine of Rioja
> nor the Galician shellfish
> nor the pastures of Castilla.
>
> Pilgrim, who is calling you?
> What hidden force at you pulls?
> Not the people of the Camino
> nor the customs of the rurals.
>
> It is not history and culture,
> nor the rooster of La Calzada
> nor Gaudi's palace
> nor the Castle of Ponferrada.

I see everything in passing
and it's a joy to see it all,
but the voice that beckons me
much more deeply I feel the call.

The force that pushes me onward
the force that pulls me in tow,
Not even I can explain it
Only the One from Above can know!

I don't know who wrote the poem or why they painted it on that wall. After I read the poem, I took off my pack, dug out my journal, and copied it down. I also took a picture of the poem on the wall, which seems redundant I guess, but there was something about the act of rewriting the poem in my journal that I felt was important to do. It was all that I wrote in my journal that day. I put my journal and my camera back in my bag and hoisted my pack back on my shoulders and continued on the road. I continued to ponder the questions that the wall had asked me. Who is calling me? What hidden force is pulling at me? I guess I didn't write any more in my journal that day because I did not have any answers. Or maybe I did, but the answer was not something I could put into words.

I have been asked a few times since I walked the Camino if I had a "mystical experience." I usually wince at this question, because I am not sure what they mean by "mystical." If they are thinking of the Shirley MacLaine kind of experience of reliving past lives that she wrote about in her book about her pilgrimage on the Camino, then no. If they are talking about the Paulo Coelho kind of experience of seeking a magical sword for some secret ritual that he wrote about in his book on the Camino, then also no.

What do people mean by a "mystical" experience? Richard Rohr defines what it means to be a mystic in his book The Naked Now and asks that we not let the word "mystic" scare us off. He explains that a mystic "simply means one who has moved from mere belief systems or belonging systems to actual inner experience. All spiritual traditions agree that such a movement is possible, desirable, and available to everyone.... Some call this movement conversion, some call it enlightenment, some transformation, and some holiness." (Rohr, p. 30)

So, how and when do these "mystical moments" happen? According to Rohr, "It happens whenever, by some wondrous 'coincidence,' our heart space, our mind space, and our body awareness are all simultaneously open and nonresistant." He calls this presence. He explains that "it is experienced as a moment of deep inner connection and it always pulls you, intensely satisfied, into the naked and undefended now, which can involve both profound joy and profound sadness. At that point, you either want to write poetry, pray or be utterly silent." (Rohr, p. 28)

If mystical experiences inspire us to write poetry, then I would think many people have had mystical experiences along the Camino de Santiago. This poem that I saw on the wall on the way from Navarette to Najera was not the only poem I found along the way. There were many places where people had left messages, often in verse, for other pilgrims to read. Some were on paper left tucked behind a statue in a grotto, or etched on a wooden fence. Some were graffiti on the inside wall of a pedestrian tunnel, and some were written in ink on post-it notes left on road signs. The Camino seems to turn pilgrims into poets. One pilgrim-turned-poet shared his poem with me after days of walking together. There was a group of us sitting around inside a hostel reflecting on our experiences on the road, when a young pilgrim named Matt asked if he could share a poem he had just written. This is the poem he shared:

Sometimes I take to wondering,
But only with a clear head and
Seem to make sense of something,
The world even (despite my blundering).

Mind my words and phrases as a part
Of me that no one will understand;
Not me, I've only begun to start
Transcending the limen between me and my heart,

Heart liminally kept: left on the right side, it separates me from I.
And I am the piece of me that I don't command,
Perhaps I am the face of a rebel, dissented from, haunted by
My rebellion, against me, within me at all times

War-- in my mind waged for my mind;
I hold myself for ransom, demand:
Attention, power, love of one kind
Or another. I am searching for something to find.

And yet hopefully I am walking,
Hoping that I'll persevere, worries crunch like sand
Underfoot, under blister, under stocking.
My hope drowned the rain, my mind drowned in talking.
Hopefully I walk forward... I subconsciously strand
A new way of life on this travelers' land.

We all clapped when he finished and thanked him for sharing and then we all sort of sat in silence for a moment afterwards, thinking about his words. Later, I asked if he minded if I could have a copy of his poem, and he graciously obliged. What is it about poetry that touches you in a way that makes you want to sit with the words, digest them, and revisit them again and again? Perhaps there is something "mystical" in writing this way. And perhaps hearing it or reading it helps move you towards an "actual inner experience" or at least witness such an experience in another. Listening to Matt's poem, I can't help but think that his experience along the Camino was in some way transformative.

I think again back to the poem on the wall. When the poet asks us what force is pulling on us, do they mean the same kind of pull that Rohr is talking about? Maybe this poet had a mystical experience and that is what moved them to write poetry on the wall. Perhaps it is because I am not a poet, or perhaps I wasn't looking for some kind of "mystical" experience, but whatever the reason, I have answered, "no" when asked if I experienced anything "mystical."

But I do believe there was a force pulling on me as I walked the Camino. This force allowed me to push through pain and keep walking. This force was pulling at me to connect with a destiny that was waiting for me. While I walked the Camino, I could feel my heart space, my mind space, and my body awareness were all simultaneously open and nonresistant. So perhaps, if I use Rohr's definition, I did have a mystical experience. This hidden force I felt was love, and who is to say that experiencing love is not something mystical?

Love is a powerful force, and I think that it is all too often overlooked, underestimated, or taken for granted. The word "love" is overused, and mostly improperly, in today's world, I think. Love is really hard to explain in words. But you know it when you see it, and by that, I mean you know love is there by how you see others react by the force it has on them. Like gravity, you can't see it, but when the apple falls from the tree, you know that it exists. Well, love is kind of like that. When you see a mother work three jobs so that she can provide for her kids, you see the love. When you see a teenager visit a sick grandparent in the hospital instead of going to a party with friends, you see the love. When you see a sister undergo surgery to give up one of her kidneys to save her brother, you see the love. When you stand at the altar and swear that you will stand by your partner's side no matter what, sickness or health, richer or poorer, and that only death can keep you apart, you see the love.

Love was difficult for me. It was not a word shared with one another much in my family growing up. I was wary of it. But I did witness love in other places. I saw it in my extended family and in my friends. It took me a long time, though, to be open to it coming into my life and being "present" for love to take me where it would. And when I left that church in Chestnut Hill that day after confession, it wasn't long before love came back into my life. Julie helped me find love again, and I believe I helped her do the same after she, too, was wary of it.

It was love that was the force pulling on me as I walked the Camino. It was the force that let me know that I was going to do whatever I needed to do to get to Santiago. If I got blisters, I would bandage them. If my knees gave out, I would get braces. If I couldn't walk anymore, I would take a bus. Whatever it took, I was going to get to Santiago with Julie and swear on the altar that I would love her for the rest of her life. Love is mystical. It is a force you cannot see, but it can pull on you with an unparalleled strength in nature. So maybe I did have a mystical experience. Maybe someday I will write a poem on a wall.

The Roasted Chicken

I hobbled into the *refugio* in Santo Domingo de la Calzada on the twenty-second of June and met my third American along the Camino, a guy in his early fifties, maybe. He was standing at the entrance to the refugio; an old stone building that could have been a converted monastery that lay in the shadow of the tower of the town's cathedral that soared into the sky connecting the cobblestone street to the clouds above. He must have recognized me as a fellow American from my face or from my dress, or that way that we Americans walk or carry ourselves, but whatever it was, he came right up to me and asked the most peculiar question.

"Is your name Adam?"

Whoa. That was weird. It is one thing for a complete stranger to guess your nationality, but completely another to guess your first name. Who was this guy and how did he know my name? As I stood there stunned and before I could answer, he followed up with

"Are you getting married in Santiago?"

"Uhhh...errr...yes," I stuttered, not knowing if I was perhaps divulging more information than I should. But before I could ask how he knew this, he told me that he had heard from another pilgrim, one he was walking with a few days earlier, that there was an American walking the Camino with the intention of meeting his fiancée along the road and then getting married when they arrived in Santiago and that the American's name was Adam.

He introduced himself and told me his name was Jim Callahan from California. Like me, Jim had not seen many Americans on the road, so when he saw me approaching, he guessed that I might be that guy he heard about. He described the pilgrim who told him my story, but I did not recognize that person from his description. All I can guess is that I was telling my story to someone along the way, who then told someone else about me, and perhaps passed the story on a few more times before it reached Jim. What was entertaining to me was that my story arrived at Santo Domingo de la Calzada before I did!

I thought about the people I had walked with so far and how my story might have traveled along. There was Takeshi Hirazuka, a Japanese *hostalero* in Navarette that spoke Spanish with a Castilian lisp. There was Evan the Asian-American student from North Carolina who just finished his AP Spanish Literature exam and planned to go to Georgetown University when he returned with hopes of taking a class with former Spanish president José María Aznar. There was Joanna, a short, spikey-haired German woman, and there was Nayera the bartender from Los Arcos. There were so many different people, and so many different languages, that for my story to move so quickly along the Camino from pilgrim to pilgrim and arrive in tact, was something short of a miracle.

I had a hunch that one link in the chain was Peter, the guy from Germany who was the rare German who spoke no English, nor any Spanish for that matter. I met him on the way to Azofra at a café. He waved at me and asked,

"Welcher Tag ist es?"

Now, I studied German for one year as a ninth grader in high school, but that was some twenty-odd years ago. I think he wanted to know what day was it, so I tried remembering my numbers, but couldn't get past nineteen, and it was the twenty-first, so I just held up my fingers. I did remember how to say *"Ich bin ein Hamburger"* which means, I'm from Hamburg, and I always thought that was funny because it sounds like I am saying that I am a hamburger! I was born in Hamburg, so it is true.

Well, I don't know if he was just excited that I was trying to speak German, but he responded very emphatically saying that he, too, was from Hamburg...I think. He and I walked for a while that day in the same fashion that Toshi and I did a few days before. We took turns talking and pretending to understand what the other said. I spoke in English because I figured that was closer to German than Spanish was. When we arrived at Azofra, I said I needed to stop, but he indicated he was going on to the next town and we parted ways. The next day was when the miracle of tongues occurred. I was walking by myself through the town when I saw Peter sitting at a café having breakfast. He waved me over enthusiastically and told me how nice the albergue was where he stayed that night.

The *hospitaleros* were extremely hospitable. They brought his backpack upstairs for him and could speak many languages including German. Also, they had a small pool of cool water in the back yard for bathing your feet. He was so happy there that he decided he would spend another night. Now, Peter said all this in German, and I know that my memory of first year German from decades ago was not sufficient enough for me to understand all this, and I doubt I even learned all this vocabulary in the first place. Yet, somehow, I understood everything he said...mostly. How do I know? Because at the next table over was Bridget, a German woman whom I met a couple days earlier who also spoke English.

I asked her if what I understood from Peter was correct,

and she said it was...mostly. I guess a lot of meaning can be deduced from context, and there are similarities between German and English, but whatever the explanation of how I understood Peter that morning, I like to chalk it up to one of the "miracles" along the Camino.

I had walked for a while with Bridget that other day. She was with Francesca, Enrique and Alejandro, an Italian, and two Spaniards respectively, all in their early twenties. I am guessing they also had something to do with passing my story along. They were walking together, but I am guessing the two women met up with the two Spanish fellows along the way, as Enrique was from Avila and Alejandro was from Logroño, which is right on the leg of the Camino we were walking. Alejandro said they actually stayed at his house the night before I met them and were up partying until six in the morning. They said they were planning on taking it easy that day.

I assumed this was not unusual for some pilgrims, because I had recently passed a bar along the road called *"La Resaca"* which is translated to "The Hangover." I know I told them about my wedding plans, because I distinctly remember Enrique chiming in about his uncle's bachelor party. He said his uncle is now famous in his town for his bachelor party when he had to *"follar una cerda."* As my eyes widened in horror, I had to confirm that I understood his Spanish. Yup, he actually said his uncle became, shall we say, "intimate" with a local farmer's sow. I didn't walk with that foursome after Najera.

I am still not entirely sure if Enrique was serious or just wanting to have a little fun with this American, who for all intents and purposes was having his bachelor party alone on pilgrimage, but whatever the case, I think Enrique and Alejandro were walking the Camino in search of a fiesta more than anything else.

There was of course Vicente and Antonio, the one in the gray cassock, but I had not seen them in quite a few days. I am sure Mary and Geraldine, the two Irish ladies must have played some part in passing my story along, because I kept running into them at different points along the road, and we would chat. I know they told me that they had their luggage brought from *refugio* to *refugio* by taxi, but I couldn't figure out how I kept running into them, for as slow as my pace was, those two were more on a saunter than any kind of hike. They confessed they had taken a bus on a number of occasions when they got tired. I imagined a number of possible routes my story may have taken, but however it got there, my story found Jim before I did.

Jim invited me to stay that night at the *refugio* where he was staying, and there were plenty of beds left. I was not planning on any more walking that day, so I happily took him up on the invitation and didn't even bother looking in my guidebook to see what other lodging options were in town. I was shown into a big drafty room with metal bed frames and bare mattresses lined up against the stone walls, looking more like a field hospital than a hotel. I imagined what this room looked like centuries ago as medieval pilgrims came through looking for lodging and needing tending to their ailments, and I doubt it looked much different then. This particular *refugio* dates back to the twelfth century and was called the Cofradía del Santo, or the Brotherhood of the Saint.

The saint in question was Domingo García who dedicated his life to caring for pilgrims along the Camino, and another word for road in Spanish is *calzada*, which is derived from *calzar*, which means covering the foot with a shoe. Certainly, in Domingo García's day, most of the travelers along the road were on foot. So, this town, Santo Domingo de la Calzada, was named for him. I often wonder how someone attains sainthood. Clearly, Domingo García was a kind man who dedicated himself to the service of others, but is that enough? In the Catholic Church there is a very prescribed method for becoming a saint, and I believe part of it is performing a miracle. Well, I soon learned about one of the miracles that Domingo García performed.

After I got myself settled in the *refugio*, I went out to explore the town; primarily to find where the nearest restaurant was that was offering a *menú de peregrino*. But before I found a place to eat, I strolled into the cathedral that was right next door to look around. While the bell tower of this particular cathedral was impressive, I was not expecting to be overwhelmed by the inside, as I kind of felt I had already seen my fair share of churches along the way and how special could one more be?

Well, just as I was getting adjusted to the peaceful solitude of the silent stone interior that many of these cavernous churches have, a piercing crow of a rooster from right above my head gave me quite a startle. Looking around to see where the noise came from, I discovered something I had never seen in any other church in my life. Built into the architecture of the church above the pews was an ornate, gold-plated chicken coop, complete with a live white rooster and white hen residing inside. I learned that these two birds were direct descendants of the miraculous chickens of Saint Dominic of the Road or Santo Domingo de la Calzada.

As the legend goes, a German family was making the pilgrimage back in the fourteenth century and stayed in a hostel in this town. The daughter of the Spanish *hostaleros* was smitten by the handsome son of the German couple, but the young lad rejected her advances, as he was dedicated to the holiness of his pilgrimage. Hell hath no fury like a woman scorned, they say, and so the Spanish girl planted a silver cup in the young man's bag and then accused him of stealing.

Laws were not kind in those days and he was tried and hanged by the local authorities for being a thief. When the parents went to retrieve their son's body from the gallows, they heard the voice of their son, who was apparently still alive, saying that he was saved by Santo Domingo, who in spirit form came and held up his body to save the innocent pilgrim. The two German parents rushed to the town magistrate to tell him what happened and to have their son released from the noose. The uncaring magistrate, not wanting to be interrupted from his dinner responded to the couple by saying,

"Your son is about as alive as the roasted chicken on my plate!"

It was at uttering those words that the chicken leapt up from his plate, and squawked off the table. While I certainly cannot attest to the truth of any of this legend, there are clearly those who maintain the honor of the chickens of the cathedral of Santo Domingo de la Calzada, *dónde cantó la gallina después de asada.*

With this story fresh in my head, I opted not to have the roasted chicken on the nearby restaurant's menú de peregrino. I was about to go ask the hospitalero if there was an Italian restaurant in town, as I was having a craving for pasta for some reason, when I noticed the outdoor café right across the street was... miraculously...a *restaurante italiano.* I had tortellini with ricotta cheese and spinach and two glasses of a very nice local Rioja wine.

I could have used Santo Domingo's healing powers that night as I had one of the most restless nights of sleep due to the pain in my knee. If I moved in the slightest while sleeping, I would feel a sharp twinge of pain from my knee. I tried wedging a towel under my leg to prop my knee in a comfortable position, but even that would not stop the pain for long. The metal bed frame would squeak every time I moved trying to move my leg into a more comfortable position. Finally, I decided to move the mattress to the floor so I would not wake the other pilgrims. The mattress on the floor also provided better stability for my leg. Whether it was my new sleeping position or the six hundred milligrams of ibuprofen that a pilgrim from Mallorca gave me earlier in the evening that were finally kicking in, I finally got a couple hours of sleep.

Morning came as a relief from the pain of trying to stay still throughout the night. It took me almost five minutes to just straighten out my leg and get my knee braces on, as the slightest move would aggravate the tendons in my right knee. As I was preparing for the day's walk, a Frenchman came over to me and asked for my advice on the best way to deal with blisters. I was flattered, as I must have appeared, to him at least, as an experienced pilgrim!

I did have a pretty good routine. I would start each day by applying the deodorant stick to my feet to keep them cool and dry as possible, and this seemed to help. At night, if I had a blister, I would pop it and drain it, and in the morning apply a second-skin bandage I had acquired in a pharmacy along the Camino for just this purpose. He thanked me for my advice and went to tend to his *ampollas*. For my part, I got my things together, grabbed my stick, which I needed right away to help me walk, and headed out of the *refugio* in search of breakfast.

While other days I would try to get a good distance along the road in the early morning hours before looking for something to eat, this morning took so much exertion to walk, that I only got about a block before I decided to hobble into the *Cervecería* Titanic to sit and at least get a cup of coffee. I went up to the bar to order my coffee and saw half a *tortilla española*, the potato omelet that had become a staple for me along the pilgrimage, sitting behind the glass. I asked for a slice. The proprietor asked if I would mind waiting, because he was about to make a fresh one, and that one had been sitting in the case since yesterday. I happily obliged and took the opportunity to sit casually at a table with my leg raised on a chair and sip my coffee.

I watched this hospitable barman peel and dice the potatoes, slowly cook them in oil until soft, remove them to a bowl and mix them together with beaten eggs, onion and salt and return the mixture to the frying pan. Then he performed the most deft maneuver of the tortilla-making process, which is to cover the pan with a plate, flip the tortilla over, and then slide it back to the pan to finish cooking on the other side. He carried this out with such agility that he clearly was an expert, and I knew this was going to be one tasty tortilla. It was delicious, and with a slice of fresh baguette on the side, I took my time savoring this most typical of Spanish meals.

As I sat there in the bar, I thought about what my physical therapist told me years before when I was rehabbing from a dislocated disk in my spine.

"Forget about the saying No Pain, No Gain...pain," he said, "is your body's way of telling you that you are doing something wrong and you should stop."

Well, the pain in my knee was screaming at me to stop, but if I was to stay on track with my plan to get to Santiago in time for my wedding, then I had to keep going. There was this voice inside me egging me on, telling me I had to push through and that I if I didn't keep walking, I would feel like I had failed somehow. As I finished my breakfast, and reflected on what I had written in my journal about the "pace" of the pilgrimage, I remember thinking that I shouldn't feel pressured to keep pace with others or some preconceived notion about how long the pilgrimage should take. I wrote down the need to take care of myself so that I wouldn't find myself limping down the aisle on my wedding day. And just as I wrote those words, I saw a man pushing himself by my table in a wheelchair. Whether it was the irony of sitting in a café named after the Titanic, the unsinkable ship that sank, the omen of the man in the wheelchair, or the spirit of Santo Domingo de la Calzada speaking to me, I decided then and there that I needed a day or two of rest to let my knees heal. I would not continue walking that day.

The Bag of Frozen Peas

I would not be the first pilgrim to have to leave the Camino due to physical ailments. The two Irish ladies, Geraldine and Mary, called it quits. They knew it was the right thing to do, but they regretted having to return home to their younger relatives who would greet them with an "I told you so."

They also told me of a young Belgian woman named Naya who went to the hospital with such bad blisters that she lost two layers of skin. The doctors were less than sympathetic and chastised her for inflicting such pain on herself. There was an Irish guy named Gary who had to stop because his knee gave out, and I had yet to see Gizan, the older Japanese guy who went to the hospital before Logroño and then took a bus the next two stages. There was a young Chinese woman, walking in sneakers instead of boots, who had twisted her ankle and was hobbling with a makeshift stick she had found. It was definitely not one of Marcelino's. I don't know if she will make it, and I wonder about the young Frenchman who got bitten by the dog, if he would be able to carry on with his mother, or if they would need to bail out and tend to the unexpected wound.

Having a first aid kit with you can be a help, but you don't want to carry too much, again, to minimize the weight of the pack. The Camino is dotted with *farmacias,* marked by illuminated green crosses above the doors, along the way where you can get what you need, and can help with a quick diagnosis. According to the guide I had, blisters were the number one affliction that caused pilgrims to abandon the journey, or at least take time out to seek medical help. Next, was tendonitis. They say misery loves company, and I must admit there was comfort in knowing of all these others who had to decide to stop walking and that I was not the only one. I was not going to end my journey, but I needed a break if I was going to be able to walk with Julie when she arrived.

I not only had to rethink my pilgrimage route schedule, but also had to figure out where to stay and rest. Most hostels ask that pilgrims leave by nine in the morning, and don't expect they will stay more than a night. So, I decided to leave the Camino and take a bus back to Madrid and recuperate at my friend Antonio's apartment. I texted him on the Nokia mobile phone he had given me when I arrived in Spain, and told him of my plan. He was in the middle of taking exams for teacher recertification, but was happy to have me stay with him as long as I needed.

It was pretty easy getting there. I took the 9:15am bus to Burgos and there caught the 11:00am bus to Madrid. On the ride to Burgos, I sat next to a young woman named Kate, who told me she was studying in Finland and writing her master's thesis on the human geography of the Camino de Santiago. As we talked, I commented that her English was excellent.

"That's because I am from North Carolina!" she replied with an ironic grin.

I felt foolish that I just assumed she was from Finland and not just studying there, but she had what, to me, sounded like a European accent, and not your stereotypical southern accent. I taught for years with an assistant principal from North Carolina, and Kate sounded nothing like her. Kate said she had taught in Thailand and in Madrid, so perhaps being an expatriate for so long, she acquired a new accent. In any case, she told me about her research and she was focusing on what she called "The Camino Rat Race."

She thought it rather ironic that so many people come to Spain to walk the Camino de Santiago for the sole purpose of getting away from their daily grind at home, and yet, while on pilgrimage they recreate a pressure filled routine for themselves focused on getting up early enough to beat other pilgrims to the showers or get a jump on the trek for that day. They meticulously plan their route so that they are assured of a place to stay and that they arrive in time so that a bed is available. They seek out the restaurant with the most economical menú del peregrino and make sure they are seated in time for that meal which often is only offered during a short window of time.

Many pilgrims she interviewed have just substituted one rat race for another, and she was postulating what this desire to be part of a rigid schedule, even when you were consciously trying to escape from one, said about the human condition. I told her about my plan, and the need to arrive in Santiago by July eighth, but it was my wedding date that was driving my need to be "on time." I told her that I would soon be meeting up with Julie, but our plan to meet was in the process of being changed, due to the tendonitis in my knees. I realized then, that I had not told Julie yet that I had veered off the Camino. Keeping that little nugget of information to myself would turn out to be instrumental for when Julie arrived in Spain in a couple of days.

When I finally arrived in Madrid, I took the metro from the bus station to Chamartin, which was a train station only a couple of blocks from Antonio's apartment. Much like when I was in the airport at JFK, a pilgrim with a backpack and walking stick feels pretty out of place taking public transportation. I imagine people were wondering what I was doing on a bus or the metro when I should be walking the ancient road in the north. I got a few looks from people, but nobody ever asked. Around the corner from the apartment was a convenience store, so I stopped in to buy some groceries for the next couple of days, so that I wouldn't overly impose on Antonio's hospitality. I came across a bag of frozen peas in the freezer section and thought that would be perfect ... not to prepare a meal, but rather to put on my knees to treat the inflammation.

I remembered a few years back when I was coaching softball, I showed up to one of my player's home after she got hit in the eye with a batted ball and offered her a pint of ice cream and a bag of frozen peas. I told her that she could eat one and put the other on her eye, and it was up to her which one to choose. She opted to eat the ice cream, clearly. But the idea of putting a bag of frozen peas on my knees right then was just what the doctor ordered, so I bought the bag of frozen peas.

I spent the entire next day on Antonio's couch with peas on my knees. I did some laundry, some stretching exercises, and watched the Lord of the Rings trilogy in Spanish. It's funny how references to that movie keep coming up. Well, considering that the basic premise of those movies is a long journey on foot carrying a ring, and I was on a long journey on foot to get a ring...a wedding ring...the connection is kind of ironic. Sure, there are a lot of battle scenes, especially in the second two movies, but it really is all about the journey. And much like Frodo needed to take a few days off from walking as he convalesced with the Elves; I too needed some healing time. And as I sat there on Antonio's couch, with a bag of frozen peas on my knees, I thought back to another time and another couch when I had to exit from my daily journey to heal.

It was some five years earlier when I would find myself

recovering on my mother's couch in her townhouse in Arlington, Virginia. That time, however, a bag of frozen peas would not have helped. It was what was in a plastic prescription bottle that I needed to recover, because I did not have tendonitis, but rather I was diagnosed with clinical depression. It may seem odd that we are this far into my story and I have not mentioned my depression. Talking about physical injuries like blisters and tendonitis is much easier. It is pretty clear what causes them, and how they are treated is pretty well established.

Physical injuries are almost like a badge of honor along the Camino de Santiago, because somehow this kind of suffering is supposed to be part of the experience, part of the challenge of the pilgrimage. But talking about mental illness is an entirely different story. There is a stigma attached to suffering from mental illness that suffering from physical injuries does not seem to carry. I guess because we do not understand mental illness as well. The causes and the treatment are not as clear-cut, and despite the many advances in medical research, we still don't really understand how the brain works. So, when we hear of people suffering from mental illness, we tend to get scared rather than sympathetic. I know I was scared when I first heard that I might need psychiatric help.

I was living on my own in an apartment in Pennsylvania and working as a teacher. I loved my job and had a good group of friends, and as far as I was concerned, things were going really well in my life. But I found myself becoming increasingly tired and lacking energy. I was sleeping a lot more and was having trouble motivating myself to do the things I normally enjoyed doing. I decided I should see a doctor. My doctor did everything he could think of to diagnose what was causing this lack of energy. He ran blood tests and even ordered an MRI to scan my brain. When he could find no causes for my symptoms, he suggested I see a psychiatrist. Just the mention of the word "psychiatrist" made me uncomfortable and so I decided to just wait and see if this lethargy would eventually just go away. It didn't. Not only did I continue to feel tired, but I grew increasingly anxious about dealing with other people. I found my thoughts were growing more negative and I couldn't explain why. One day while driving home from work, the thought crossed my mind that if I drove off the road and got killed in a car accident then I wouldn't have to worry about these feelings anymore. That was when I knew I needed help. I knew that there was no reason for me to have such dark thoughts, and yet there they were. I made an appointment to see a psychiatrist the next day.

Let me be clear, making an appointment to get professional help did not suddenly make things get better. In fact, they continued to get worse. I found that despite being constantly tired, I couldn't fall asleep. My thoughts kept racing and kept me up at night, and as a result, I had trouble getting up in the morning and had trouble thinking clearly during the day. I often found myself just staring into space, trapped in my thoughts, and unable to put any of these thoughts into words. I had a hard time just carrying on simple conversations with other people, even my friends. The doctor gave me a prescription for paroxetine and klonapin, and suggested I take time off work as we figured the right dosage. I took a medical leave of absence, which was good, because I would not have been an effective teacher. I remember how difficult it was to tell my friends what was going on, but they were all so supportive.

When I went to tell the head of human resources at my school, I was surprised how nonchalant he was about my request. He explained that this was a more common condition than I might think and that I was certainly not the first teacher in the school district to make such a request. He assured me that I would not lose my job and that my benefits would cover my expenses. I ended up taking a month off, and in that time, I decided I needed someone to take care of me. As supportive as my friends were, I knew it could not be them. I called my mom, and told her what was going on and that I needed to stay with her for a week.

Normally my mom was not my go-to for support, but given the conversations I had with my psychiatrist, I felt spending some time with my mom was the right thing to do. I guess I should not have been surprised when my mom told me that she too was taking an antidepressant that her doctor had prescribe for her. It's funny how you don't know what others are dealing with until you are honest about your own issues. I had talked in therapy sessions about my mom's drinking, but I did not know that she was also diagnosed with depression. Perhaps her drinking was just her way of self-medicating. I was glad to have spent that week on my mom's couch as it definitely gave me some insight into what I was going through, and I believe it was a bit of a breakthrough for my relationship with her. I decided I should see if my dad's couch would offer the same benefits, so I called him to let him know I was coming for a visit.

I flew out to Arizona for a week, and guess what I found out there? My father also suffered from depression. In fact, he told me about a time when he attempted suicide. It was when we were living in New Jersey and my parents were still married. A neighbor of ours took her own life by carbon monoxide poisoning from car exhaust in her garage, and apparently when my dad heard about it, he tried the same thing. Fortunately, he changed his mind and opened the garage door before it was too late. It is funny the things you learn from people when you lay your soul bare to them and ask for help. Knowing that both of my parents suffered from depression might have been helpful as I was dealing with my own major depressive disorder, don't you think?

There are some studies that suggest clinical depression can be hereditary, but for me, just knowing that others in my family had experience dealing with this was, in some strange way, comforting. After two weeks of couch therapy with my parents, I returned to my apartment in Pennsylvania and got ready to go back to teaching. While I think these family breakthroughs were important to my healing, I believe the medications finally began to have the intended effect and helped level out my mood disorder. I stopped taking the klonapin after about a month, but I am still on paroxetine, albeit a much lower dosage. So, as I sat on Antonio's couch thinking about how I would carry a bag of frozen peas with me as I continued walking to treat my knees, I was reassured that the plastic bottle of antidepressants, that I made certain to get an extra prescription for before I left on this month-long pilgrimage, was safely packed and with me to help me treat my other medical condition.

You may be wondering now if Julie knew about my depression. The answer is yes. In fact, I told her about it that summer night in Boston after watching the movie in the air-conditioned theater. I didn't tell her in the theater. That would have been weird. I told her when we went back to her apartment, but I knew then that I was serious about our relationship. I also knew that finding out about a mental illness could be a deal-breaker, so I wanted to give her full disclosure in case she started to have serious feelings for me. I was nervous about telling her. So, when she took the news in stride, thanking me for being honest, and then still wanting to make out that night in the apartment, I was very relieved.

Now as I sat on Antonio's couch, I was thinking about how Julie was nervous. She was nervous about arriving in Spain by herself, not because she wasn't an experienced traveler, but because the first person she would meet would be Antonio, who did not speak English, and she wasn't super confident in her Spanish. Couple the language barrier with jet lag, and having to make four hours' worth of small talk in a long car ride with someone you have only met once... well...it would not be the ideal first day in Spain for Julie.

She was to fly to Madrid after connecting in Málaga, because that was the only route that Air Plus Comet flew. Yes, the name of the airline we both traveled on was called Air Plus Comet. It was the cheapest ticket by far that we could find on Travelocity, but even I was skeptical it was a real airline. I did a web search and found articles touting how the Prince of Asturias flew on an Air Plus Comet flight, which I think was orchestrated to ensure travelers that it was a safe airline. So, for five hundred dollars round trip, we booked our flights, albeit for different departure dates. Her flight was to arrive on the twenty-sixth. The plan was for Antonio to pick her up from the airport and then drive her to meet me in León, which would have been about a four-hour car ride.

Truth be told, I think Antonio was a bit uncomfortable, too. When he returned to his apartment the day before Julie was to arrive, we had dinner and discussed the itinerary for the next couple of days. He came up with a rather ingenious plan that took advantage of the fact that I was unexpectedly in Madrid, which would both alleviate the rather awkward time that he and Julie would have to spend alone together in the car and add to the romance of her arrival.

This was Antonio's idea: he would meet Julie at the airport and act like I was in León waiting for her as planned. I would hide with my phone while he called me to let me know Julie arrived. He would put her on the phone so we could talk, and while I pretended to be in León, I would say something clever to make her turn around and she would see

I was really right there in the airport waiting for her. Then there would be this big emotional moment where we would run towards each other in slow motion and embrace in a long, romantic-movie-like kiss. That was the plan.

Well, when we got to the airport, we waited, and waited, and waited. The flight kept changing the time of arrival. Apparently, Air Plus Comet only had one plane and it was delayed in Málaga before arriving in Madrid. She had to clear customs there before coming to Madrid, as that was the international port of entry. When the plane finally landed in Madrid, Julie exited the gate and Antonio went up to meet her while I waited outside. As they walked out, I hid behind a pillar and Antonio suggested they call me to let me know she had arrived. My phone rings and he hands the phone to Julie to talk. I ask her how she's doing, and she said she was OK, but a little tired. I said she looked good to me...and she paused and said,

"How would you know?"

I chuckled, and said, "Well, from where I'm standing..."

She turned around and saw me behind her smiling with the phone to my ear. A look of joy and relief came across her face and she came into my arms and we held each other tight. Cue the long, romantic-movie-like kiss. I don't know which of the three of us was most relieved in this moment, but the car ride back to the Camino went better than anyone had expected. Antonio could speak in Spanish knowing I was there to help interpret. Julie sat in the back and was able to relax from her flight. And I was off my feet for another few hours and was bypassing a few hundred kilometers of the pilgrimage route that I wouldn't have to walk. We ended up skipping León entirely, but my detour to Madrid was exactly what the doctor had ordered...that, and a bag of frozen peas.

The Snail

As I sat in the passenger seat of Antonio's blue Seat coupe watching the Spanish countryside whiz by me on our way from Madrid to Ponferrada, I couldn't help but think about all the things I had seen on my journey thus far that I could never have seen if I had been making that trek by car. On foot, you catch details of nature that are impossible to process speeding past them at eighty to one hundred kilometers per hour. From the highway, everything is a blur. On foot, everything is under a microscope.

One day when I had been walking by myself, I came across something that even on foot was easy to miss. In fact, I almost stepped on it without knowing. Right there in the middle of the path was a snail. I saw it midstride just before my boot came down on it, and I stopped suddenly. I slowly took off my pack to find my camera, so I could capture this natural phenomenon right before me. Now I know you are thinking, "What is so special about a snail?"

Well first of all, I don't know that I had ever seen a snail moving along in its natural habitat before. I had seen them in aquariums, as animated creatures in movies, and on the menu in fancy restaurants, but not just trekking along with its home on its back in no hurry to get to where it's going. Where was it going? Based on its current trajectory and speed of travel, it might not make it to the other side of the road before the end of the day. Even less a chance of getting that far if some unobservant pilgrim comes clomping by and crushes it under boot. I got out my camera, bent down low, and snapped a picture. This picture of nature caught in an unexpected moment was not going to make the cover of National Geographic, but I wanted to have a memory of that snail. I wanted to acknowledge, first, that there was some creature moving slower than I was.

Before coming upon this tireless monopod traveler, I was just thinking that my pace had been slowing over the past few kilometers. I could feel my steps getting shorter and I found myself leaning more on my walking stick than I had been earlier in the day. My legs were getting tired; the blister on my left pinky toe was beginning to whine, and my knees were beginning to throb. As I hobbled along, other pilgrims passed me with the compulsory nod and call of *"Buen Camino."*

I started thinking about how slow I was walking and whether or not I should pick up the pace. Would pushing through the pain be better if I went faster and got the day's journey over quicker, or would it be better to slow down even if it meant staying on my feet longer. The distance would be the same, so would the pace matter? It made me think about how as a kid, I would run through the rain thinking I would somehow get less wet. I wondered if that was true or if you get the same amount of wet, just faster? In any case, while pondering how slow I was walking, I came upon that snail...as if to remind me everything is relative. Quicker is not necessarily better. And just as the saying on the little blue bracelets in the souvenir shops with yellow lettering reminds us *"El Camino es la meta."* The journey is the goal.

If anyone along this pilgrimage route were really worried about when they arrive at the next stop, they could always take a bus or call a cab. In fact, all along the Camino are posted pamphlets advertising taxi services to take you or your luggage to the next *refugio*. I am not sure if they are meant to be caring lifelines in times of need or sly temptations to test a pilgrim's mettle. Most likely they are just a means of some cab driver trying to earn a living from this modern-day walking trade route. I think that little snail was there to remind me that there are lots of different paces to walk the Camino, and I should not worry too much about comparing mine with that of others.

While walking the path of The Camino, I found myself walking with a wide variety of people, and each walking at their own pace. There were women in their seventies, college kids on summer break, middle-aged business men taking a week off from work, and the list goes on. I've told you about many of them already. I met people from all parts of Spain, from France, Germany, Ireland and Italy, from Japan, and the U.S. There were people from all walks of life. When you choose to walk with someone you meet on the Camino for an extended period of time there is a certain unspoken negotiation about what pace to walk.

If your fellow pilgrim is much slower than you, then you may choose to take a more leisurely pace to maintain their company. The converse is true if they tend to walk faster, you may find yourself pushing your limits just to keep up. I found that changing my pace was difficult to maintain over an extended period of time. The problem that arose in the first scenario is that my mind started to become more conscious of my pace and I would feel an urge to move on, and I would get frustrated with my companion. This is especially true if they wanted to stop for a rest. If I was still feeling energized and I stopped, I might lose my momentum. What would happen if I could not regain my pace? What would happen if I weren't able to get to the next refugio where I planned to stay for the night? What if I arrived, but was too late, and all the beds were taken? Would I have enough energy to push on to the next town? All of these internal questions would arise as I contemplated the slower pace of my walking companion. I usually resolved this when, finding an opportune moment, I could tactfully say, "I think I am going to continue on, but I hope to see you at some point down the road." And then of course I would depart with the customary, *"Buen Camino."*

In the second scenario I would feel pressured to keep up and I would start to lose confidence in myself. Was I walking too slowly? Should I be in better shape? If I keep pushing myself, am I going to get injured? What is the rush? Will I be missing out on something if I don't keep up? I would usually resolve this problem in a similar way by saying, "I am going to take a break, but why don't you go on and I'll catch up with you at the next town." This of course would also be followed by the obligatory departing phrase, *"Buen Camino."*

It is a treat when you find someone who walks at the same pace as you, and yet you never know whom that will be until you start walking together. In many ways, finding a walking companion is like finding a good dance partner and, in some ways, like dating. You want to spend some time with them without having to commit to walking with them all the way to Santiago. And like dating, you want to get to know someone to find out if you two are compatible without having to commit to marrying them.

A horrible thought suddenly occurred to me. What if, when Julie arrived in Spain to join me on the Camino, I would find out we are not good walking companions? I have ALREADY asked her to marry me and she has ALREADY agreed! Was this me getting pre-wedding jitters? Could this perfect wedding plan turn into a reason for one of us to back out? What if Julie and I aren't in sync when we start walking together from Ponferrada to Santiago? What is it that lets you know when you and someone else are in sync with each other? Is it emotional, physical, social, chemical, spiritual? Cultural anthropologist, Edward T. Hall, talks about "being in sync" in his book Beyond Culture:

> "People in interactions either move together (in whole or in part) or they don't and in failing to do so are disruptive to others around them. Basically, people in interactions move together in a kind of dance, but they are not aware of their synchronous movement and they do it without music or conscious orchestration. Being "in sync" is itself a form of communication. The body's messages (in or out of awareness) whether read technically or not, seldom lie, and come much closer to what the person's true but sometimes unconscious feelings are than does the spoken word." (Hall, p.71)

This idea of moving together as a means of communicating seems to be at the core of the pilgrim's experience. I often found myself walking with people like Toshi, whose language I could not understand, and yet we could spend hours together in each other's company getting along fine. But I never walked with the same person for more than a day or two. I also enjoyed time walking alone. At one point while walking alone I passed two pilgrims walking together and complaining about their experiences along the Camino. They were complaining about the lodging, the food, their physical ailments, and anything that they could think of. I kept my distance because I did not want to get sucked into their gripe session. I waited for the opportunity to speed up and pass them. When they stopped for a drink of water, I quickly walked past them with the obligatory *"Buen Camino"* greeting and continued on to get far enough ahead so that their complaints faded behind me.

I thought about the age-old riddle, "If a tree falls in the

forest and no one is there to hear it, does it make a sound?" Along those lines, if you are walking the Camino by yourself, and you had no one to talk to, would you bother complaining?

Sure, my blisters were bothering me. Yeah, the last *refugio* I slept in smelled like feet and wet socks. And is it too much to ask for a shower that you can actually stand up in that also has hot water? But, walking by myself, I didn't have anyone to complain to, and what is the point anyway? If my feet hurt, then I can either decide to stop and tend to them, or continue walking. If I didn't like the smell of the place where I slept, I could find a different place or realize that my own smell might have been contributing to the odor. And while the shower was small and cold, I did get clean, and it was invigorating. I guess there are some that find comfort in complaining, or perhaps it is just their preferred way of communicating. I can't imagine walking the entire pilgrimage road having to listen to someone complaining the whole time. That would be hell. Would it be better to just walk this journey alone?

I didn't mind walking alone. Sometimes I preferred it. But to walk the entire Camino without interacting with other pilgrims would be missing the point of the whole experience. It was precisely when I engaged with my fellow pilgrims that I learned more about myself and about what I was doing out here on this pilgrimage road. In his book "No Man is an Island", Thomas Merton explains that as people look for meaning in life, they cannot merely look inward towards themselves. Yet, he points out a challenging paradox. "We cannot find ourselves within ourselves, but only in others, yet at the same time before we can go out to others, we must first find ourselves." And for those pilgrims who are out walking this road to find God, Merton presents another paradox to consider. "As for this 'finding' of God, we cannot even look for Him unless we have already found Him, and we cannot find Him unless he has first found us."

While I wasn't walking the Camino to find God, I was certainly open to some divine reassurance that I was making the right decision to get married at the end of this long walk. No, there was not some thundering voice from the clouds saying, "Go, Adam, and get married in Santiago!" But as I learned how much richer my experience walking the Camino was when I walked with others, I knew that my life would be that much richer living with someone that I love.

"We do not exist for ourselves alone, and it is only when we begin to love ourselves properly and thus also love others," explains Merton.

But Julie and I had only known each other for barely a year. What if this love that we share now fades as we get older and we see that neither of us is perfect? But marriage, like the Camino, is not a destination, it is a journey, and when you love someone, you don't just love their good qualities, you love all of them.

Merton reassures us that "if we live for others, we will gradually discover that no one expects us to be 'as gods.' We will see that we are human, like everyone else, that we all have weaknesses and deficiencies, and that these limitations of ours play a most important part in all our lives. It is because of them that we need others and others need us. We are not all weak in the same spots, and so we supplement and complete one another...." I would soon find out how well Julie and I would supplement one another as we started walking this next leg of the Camino...together.

As Antonio pulled in to the parking lot of the Hotel Madrid in Ponferrada, I reached back to touch Julie's knee to gently wake her. She had slept through most of the car ride. While the Hotel Madrid was only a three-star accommodation, it was pure luxury compared to the *refugios*

I had been staying in. Sleeping on a bunk in a hostel did not seem like the best way to recover from a long international flight, so that is why we opted for a hotel. We woke early the next morning, and after a light breakfast we parted ways with Antonio, knowing we would see him again soon in Santiago, and Julie and I headed off together on the Camino. Julie with fresh legs, and I with my rested knees were ready to start our long walk down the aisle.

The Butterflies

The countryside approaching Galicia was a welcomed change from the dry, more barren landscape of Castilla y León, but it also brought more hills. The day's walk was clicking along smoothly until we hit this fork in the road. One path turned left to go along the highway and the other headed into the woods. We looked at the guidebook and the map showed them to be about the same distance. There were arrows painted on a wall pointing in both directions so we knew that both were legitimate choices to continue following the Camino. Next to the arrow pointing right, there was writing on the wall that said, "Difficult road, for good hikers only."

I don't know if it was the desire to show Julie that my weeks of hiking the Camino had turned me into a "good hiker," or if I was more intrigued by the sights we may see along the wooded trail, but whichever it was, we chose to go right. What the map didn't show was that we had to scale a mountain. The ascent was not really that bad. Going uphill didn't seem to bother my knees. Along that road we saw for the first time the purple flowers that looked like a bunch of tiny hanging bells. I would learn later these were called Foxglove, but having no idea at the time what they were called, and given the theme of our walk, Julie and I referred to them as "our wedding bells." I took a picture to remember them, not realizing we would see plenty of them as we got closer to Santiago.

We got to the peak of the trail and started downhill, and that is when my knees reminded me that they were still there doing most of the work during this stretch of road. I stopped and turned around and faced Julie. I had an idea. I remembered Antonio's riddle from the beginning of the pilgrimage about how it is better to walk with a friend. I had to get down this mountain, but walking uphill was much kinder on the knees, so what if I walked backwards down the trail? I asked Julie to be my eyes and tell me what I was walking into so that I could proceed down while facing upwards. She agreed, and we proved Antonio's riddle right.

We walked like this for another twenty minutes or so until the road finally met up with the other path that went along the highway and the descent ended. In hindsight (excuse the pun), I think we should have gone left to walk along the highway and paid attention to the writing on the wall. Huh? How did I miss that obvious reference to the old saying about paying attention to warnings? I should have seen the writing on the wall. Nevertheless, I understood what Merton meant about supplementing each other's weak spots. Without Julie's help, I don't know how I would have made it down that incline without some serious pain.

We arrived at Vega de Valcarce, and, thanks to Julie being the eyes in the back of my head, my knees were feeling pretty good. This was a small village that only had one restaurant that we could find, and the refugio we found had a sign on the door saying the hospitalera would be there by 9pm, but that the door was open and pilgrims could go in and find an available bed in one of the rooms. The spirit of hospitality and trust one can find along the Camino never ceased to surprise me. I guess it shouldn't surprise me too much, as I tend to be a rather trusting soul as well.

We decided to stay here for the night, and as I unpacked

to get my towel and toiletries bag to go shower, I left my wallet out on the bed. I realized this as I stepped into the shower, but was more afraid of Julie seeing it than anyone taking it. She is definitely more safety conscious than I am and would give me a rash of shit for being so careless. She told me about how she would padlock her backpack to the bedframes when she and her brother traveled across the world together, and while we were not doing that on the Camino, she would most certainly not approve of me just leaving my wallet out. I know I should have learned my lesson from Cizur Menor, but again, I tend to err on the side of being overly trusting. This is just one more way that Julie is a good "supplement" for me. Taking showers in the refugios are never long ones, so I made it back in time to put away my wallet before anyone, including Julie, noticed.

It wasn't until the next morning after we bought some food for the day's walk that we noticed the old castle on the hill. It did not look inhabited; in fact, with the morning mist surrounding it, I was sure it must have been haunted. And then we heard the loud clacking sounds. We looked up as the noise seemed to be coming from above our heads. I had never heard such a sound. It was like this strange percussion instrument, as if two bamboo sticks were striking each other in rapid succession making a woody trill. We were mystified.

We were passing a church in the town and heard the noise again, only louder. There was a local woman sitting on a bench, and letting our curiosity get the best of us, we walked over to her and asked if she heard the sound. She pointed up at the top of the church and said, *"cigüeñas."* As we looked up at the stone bell tower above the church entrance, we saw a large nest with storks. Now I knew what storks were, but honestly, I had never seen a real one. I only had the cartoon version of the white bird with a sack in its mouth delivering a baby as my visual frame of reference.

These birds did not look quite as white. They definitely had gray or brown feathers mixed in, but we could see the white head with the long beak, and then, as if on cue, it clacked its beak open and closed in a rapid succession making that noise that we could not place earlier.

The local woman then followed up with this little rhyme, *"En San Blas la cigüeña verás, si no la vieres año de nieves."*

So, according to this Spanish saying, if you see storks on St. Blaise's Day, then it is an omen of good weather, because if you don't, you can expect a year with lots of snow. I guess this is the Spanish version of Groundhog Day in the United States. I reached into my bag to get my camera and snapped a photo of this miraculous bird that had eluded me throughout my life until this day. It is intriguing that I had never seen a stork before that day...that day I was walking with Julie on my way to get married. Aren't storks associated with bringing babies? Was this stork more than just an omen of good weather to come? I guess it is no wonder that we spent a good part of the day's walk thinking of names we liked for kids, if we had any.

The day's journey was mostly all uphill as we headed towards O Cebreiro. It was a beautiful walk, and the weather was great, but ironically, we had to pull out our rain jackets for the first time. You see, as we ascended into Galicia, known as the Ireland of Spain, it not only got cooler, but we encountered this unexpected fog bank, which we would soon realize was a cloud. Yes, we walked up into a cloud. And if you paid attention in fifth grade science class you would know clouds are made of water particles, so we needed our rain jackets to keep us from getting wet. We passed a stone marker that said we were officially crossing from Castilla-Leon into Galicia. And as we continued to climb, the clouds dissipated and it was sunny again. The village of O Cebreiro sits at over four thousand feet elevation, and arriving there after climbing above a cloud made it feel pretty high up. Entering the village felt like walking into the Shire from the Lord of the Rings movies. I know...again with that movie allusion! Along the windy, little, cobblestone road were scattered these thatch-roofed houses called *pallozas*, that could easily have been home to hobbits. We were so intrigued by this little hamlet nestled atop a mountain that we decided to stay the night. We found a room available for thirty-six euros in Casa Carolo, which had quaint rustic rooms with its own bathroom, which is quite the treat when you are used to the common baths of the refugios. I did have to sit or crouch in the shower because it was so small, so maybe hobbits really did live here.

We went into a café for lunch, and we saw Kate, the young woman from North Carolina that I met on the bus to Madrid, sitting by herself. She recognized me and invited us to join her. I still wondered if she was making up the part of being from North Carolina, because she clearly spoke English with more of a European accent than one from south of the Mason-Dixon line. In any case, she was a perfect plant, because when I introduced her to Julie, she said it was an honor to meet the woman I had talked so much about. She told Julie about how excited I was about taking a bus to Madrid to meet her there at the airport when she arrived. I am sure Julie knew this by seeing first-hand the excitement on my face, but it was nice to have someone else confirm my story! If it weren't for the cute freckles on her face, I would swear Julie was blushing a bit listening to Kate talk about my excitement.

After lunch Julie and I wandered up to the Santuario Santa María la Real, a small stone church that dates back to the ninth century. This was apparently the oldest church along the Camino de Santiago, which is saying a lot, because it seems the Camino is littered with old churches from

Roncesvalles to Santiago. And like many of the others, this one too had an interesting story.

Around the year 1300 a miracle occurred that was a sign from God chastising a local priest. As the legend goes, the local priest of O Cebreiro did not believe in the actual transubstantiation of the Eucharist during the mass, and one Sunday, when he assumed nobody would come to mass due to the winter storm that had set in on the hamlet, one local parishioner fought his way through the wind and snow to attend mass. The priest mocked the local man's devotion but was obliged to say mass since he had come. It is interesting that the priest plays the villain in this tale of religious devotion, and it is the common townsfolk who show their faith. So, as if God were smacking the priest on the back of his head for his cynicism, during the consecration of the host, the bread actually turned to flesh and the wine turned to blood, which stained the linen cloth under them on the table...according to the legend.

As Julie and I visited the church, we could see, there in a glass case, the legendary cup, plate and cloth on display. The literal Holy Grail, if you will, although the museum in León claims to have the Holy Grail that Jesus actually used, but I won't get into that debate. Before leaving the church, I knelt to pray, telling Julie that every time you enter a new church, you get three wishes. You can probably guess what my wishes were.

That night we slept in our own room, but heard what we could only describe as "mooing" coming from the other side of the wall. When we got up to leave Casa Carolo for our day's journey along the Camino, we were not the only ones leaving the building. A herd of cows were coming out of a large barn door at the back of the house. Apparently, we had slept next to the cows that night. And as we headed out of O Cebreiro, through the morning chill and the misty clouds, we couldn't help but be enveloped by the aroma of cows.

We had to step carefully along this stretch of the Camino, so as to avoid the patties the cows had left behind as clear reminders that pilgrims were not the only ones walking along this road. The countryside was beautiful, and Julie remarked that it reminded her of Ireland, just like it's nickname implied. And all along the path were flowers with butterflies fluttering about them. You did not want to stop too long to smell the flowers though, as pretty soon you would get a waft of cow poop.

Since walking with Julie, I found we were less likely to engage with other pilgrims along the road. I don't know if it is because others are less likely to start up conversation for fear of interrupting or if we were not as aware of others because we were so caught up in our own company. But remembering the importance of hospitality as part of the pilgrim code, I offered cookies to those passing by as Julie and I stopped for a snack and a rest. A Spanish woman stopped and graciously accepted one. While chatting with her, she pointed over my shoulder to a small brown and yellow bird that had landed on my walking stick. I fed a bit of cookie to the bird. I reached for my camera to get a picture, but as I did, it flew away. Later that day we saw three white doves nesting in ivy along a stone wall. Again, I went for my camera, and again by the time I got it, the birds had flown away. Storks are much easier to capture with a camera. I guess I could have titled this chapter "The Storks and the Bird and the Doves and the Butterflies," but that is a bit longwinded. Speaking of longwinded, I had better get to the butterfly part, since it is in the title of the chapter. Our encounter with two butterflies was a sign to me that we were making the right decision to get married.

We were walking the last leg of the day's journey when we had stopped for a drink of water and I noticed a butterfly had landed on a bush beside me. This time I reached over to the butterfly before reaching for my camera, and was surprised as the butterfly slowly crawled onto my hand. As it stayed there, I asked Julie to get the camera out and take a picture. I didn't know why the butterfly seemed so content to just sit there on my open palm until I examined it a little closer. It was missing a leg. As it moved slightly in my hand, it kind of hobbled on its remaining legs. I felt a sort of kinship with this butterfly as I too spent a good part of my pilgrimage hobbling.

After Julie took the picture, I gently returned the butterfly to the bush that I had found it in. That is when the curious event happened. Another butterfly fluttered down to the same spot and picked up the injured butterfly and slowly flew away with it. We caught a picture of the two butterflies in midflight as the one held on to the other. Julie said that the one butterfly came to save the other butterfly. I offered a less romantic point of view. I said that we probably just witnessed the act of natural copulation, although I think I used less formal terminology. I definitely like Julie's version better. And as I reflect on it now, I think it was nature's way of imitating what I had experienced along the Camino. I was hobbling along on my own, and then Julie joined me to help me finish the journey. In fact, I might even extend this metaphor beyond the Camino and say the hobbling butterfly was me living on my own before meeting Julie, and only together with her was I able to move on in my life and fly. Okay... maybe I am getting too carried away with metaphor, and sometimes butterflies are just...well, butterflies.

The Napkin

The closer we got to Santiago, the more crowded with pilgrims the road became. On our way to Vega del Valcarce we were swarmed by a school group of one hundred and eighteen students from Valladolid all walking the Camino together. I know that number sounds rather specific. We didn't actually count them ourselves. We met up with one of the teachers who was chaperoning the group who told us the exact head count. I love teaching, but chaperoning a group that big, walking the Camino, is not something I would volunteer to do. Julie and I did our best to stay ahead of them so that we wouldn't get trampled. We were able to walk at a faster pace than the flock of students, so we soon left them behind.

More pilgrims on the Camino did not just make the road more crowded to walk on, it also made finding available beds in the *refugios* more difficult. In Triacastela we stayed in a place that actually had to turn away some pilgrims. They had arrived after seven in the evening while Julie and I were doing laundry in the common room there. As they left in search of another place to stay, we heard them grumbling about the two student groups that had arrived earlier and were taking up many of the beds. These student groups were nowhere near as big as the group from Valladolid. The group of one hundred and eighteen students, however, was not competing for beds in the *refugios* because they would only stay in *polideportivos*, community centers or public gymnasiums, according to what their chaperone told us. So, as we continued our pilgrimage, we had to be more mindful about our arrival times and which towns had more lodging options. We also heard grumblings about "cheaters" from pilgrims who were turned away because there was no room in the proverbial inn.

Apparently, more and more pilgrims on this leg of Camino would send their luggage on ahead with a taxi or support van. We met one young couple, Joaquin and Ana, who were walking with Joaquin's in-laws. They kept hanging back from their family to talk with Julie and me. Joaquin said it was so he could practice his English, but I think it had more to do with wanting some space from the in-laws. They explained that they were actually walking with two support vehicles. One would carry the luggage and the other to bring Ana's pregnant sister. They also said they made reservations ahead of time, but apparently you can only do that at private albergues and not at the public *refugios*. I don't know if it is fair to call them "cheaters," but I understand the feeling of arriving at a *refugio* completely exhausted thinking your feet could not carry you one step farther, only to find out there was no room and you had to keep walking to find other lodging for the night. That happened to us.

While we had been pretty lucky so far finding beds, if you can call sleeping in the bunk under a pilgrim from Barcelona who coughed and sneezed all night and asked you for ibuprofen because he thought he had a fever, or next to a young woman from Madrid who threw up, went to the hospital, only to come back two hours later to say she was diagnosed with a bacterial infection, "lucky!" Sure, the *refugios* were cheap and they provided that "pilgrim community" that made the experience what it was, but Julie and I decided to treat ourselves to a cheap hotel outside of

Castromaior just to get a break from the "authentic charms" of the pilgrim experience in the *refugios*. Having a private room with your own shower was such a luxury. And once you stay in one of those, going back to the *refugio* grind was a bit harder. Nevertheless, that was our plan. We had planned one of our days to end at Ribadiso de Baixo, and when we got there, we were so delighted to see this picturesque little hamlet with a babbling brook to cross just before we arrived at our *refugio*. It was a long day of walking and the sun was beginning to set and our feet had told us five kilometers earlier that it was time to stop for the day. We headed up the garden path to the *refugio* that was listed in our guidebook with a glowing review only to find that it was full.

Our hearts sank. Our legs and shoulders whined. Our feet screamed, and we looked with despair at the guidebook for the next closest place of lodging. It was another three kilometers to Arzua. Now three kilometers may not seem like a long distance, but when your body ached all over and your feet and legs had carried you and your pack farther that day than they really wanted to, and knowing that you would have to pick up the pace to beat the setting sun before darkness set in, then three kilometers can seem like an impossible journey. But as we had no choice, we hoisted our packs back on our shoulders and trudged off to Arzua. We made it just as the last light of day disappeared behind the row of buildings along the main street where we found a *refugio* with available beds.

As the days of walking the Camino passed, Julie and I found our conversations turning from the sights and sounds of the pilgrimage road to sharing stories about our families; from our thoughts on heaven and God to names for our kids, if we should have any. By the time we arrived in Arzua, we were talking about the details of our wedding and what preparations we needed to make when we got to Santiago.

We were two days out, but our thoughts were already there.

When we awoke in Arzua to the first day of rain since we started our walk together, we took it as a sign. We decided to take a bus the last two legs of our journey and get to Santiago a day early to make sure we had enough time to get ready. Sure, that might put us square in the middle of the "cheaters" column, but the truth was that getting ready for our wedding was the whole point of this pilgrimage, so we were really being true to our mission. And really, we were just so excited about getting married now, that we didn't want to wait any longer.

As the rain beat down on the windows of the bus, blurring the landscape as we drove by, and as we sat dry with our packs above us in the overhead luggage racks, also dry, we knew we had made the right decision. But we were arriving in Santiago a day earlier than planned and we had not made any reservations for a place to stay that night. We did have the forethought to reserve a room for the night before and the night of the wedding, and that was pretty exciting. You see, we didn't just reserve a room in a hotel. We reserved a room in the *Parador Hostal de Los Reyes Católicos*! What is a *"parador"* you ask? Throughout Spain, historical buildings have been converted to luxury hotels so that architectural treasures and cultural landmarks can be preserved while affording tourists a unique place to stay. Some were castles, some were monasteries, and this particular parador was a hospital built by the Spanish royals back in 1499 to accommodate pilgrims traveling to Santiago. It is thought to be one of the oldest hotels in the world, and the modern royal family will stay here when they come to visit Santiago de Compostela. Sure, it was expensive, but we figured we could splurge for two nights. It was our wedding after all! But we were arriving a day early with no reservation, and we were not even considering an extra night in the *Parador Hostal de Los Reyes Católicos.*

The bus dropped us off just outside the historic center of the city and we picked up the yellow arrows painted along the sidewalks to guide us in. As we entered the old part of the city, I started to recognize my surroundings. We found ourselves in the Plaza de Cervantes and I told Julie I had stayed near there two years ago when I was studying there for the summer. I followed my nose to the dormitory of San Augustín where I had slept for three weeks back in the summer of 2002.

Julie and I entered the large ornate doorway to the converted-monastery-now-college-dorm and were greeted by a friendly face. Juan, the same guy who worked the front desk two years ago, recognized me and came up and gave me a great big hug. I remembered him of course, because we would talk each day of my stay, but he must have seen so many students come and go, that I was surprised he remembered me. He said he was expecting me, because he had heard from another former student about my plan to get married in Santiago and that I might be there sometime in July. Again, I was amazed how my story arrived before I did. After the heartfelt hugs and introducing Julie to Juan, we explained our predicament of not having a place to stay. Juan immediately thought of a hotel right in the old city just a few blocks away where he knew the owner and called to see if there was an available room. There was! We thanked Juan for his help, hugged once again, and waved good-bye.

We walked to Hotel Real, which means Royal Hotel in Spanish, and found them expecting us with a key ready. We made it. We were safe, healthy and excited to get married. Now all we needed to do was find a wedding dress for Julie, a suit for me, and a couple of wedding rings...and we had two days to do it. No problem...or so we thought.

We set off on our scavenger hunt through the

cobblestone alleyways slick from the rain, jumping to the cover of the arched *portales* that were typical of this medieval city to avoid getting wet. We first set out to find a dress for Julie. We came across a small dress shop with a dress displayed in the window that caught Julie's eye. It was a white, crocheted-lace, vintage dress that looked amazing on her. The only catch was that it needed to be taken in a bit to fit correctly. When we told the shop owner of our predicament, she was so taken by our story of the pilgrimage that she said she would do it herself that night...at no charge! We then found this salmon-colored shawl that would be perfect to keep the chill off during the evening ceremony in the stone chapel. After finding a cheap suit for me, that fit well enough off the rack to get by for one night, the next item on our list were the rings.

After the third jewelry store that we entered confirmed that there was no way we could get rings properly sized in one day, we started to get worried. So far, we had been extremely fortunate in our one-day-wedding-preparation shopping spree. The most challenging part was when I tried to explain to a lingerie shopkeeper that we needed a body suit for underneath Julie's dress, without knowing the word in Spanish. I didn't even know the word in English. Julie had to explain it to me. The funny look the shopkeeper gave me made me feel a bit like a letch as I stood their pointing to Julie and explaining I needed some underwear to cover up parts that could be seen through the dress she had just bought. Let's just say charades can be awkward when shopping for underwear! But the skeptical look quickly changed to a smile as she pulled a box from under the counter and opened up exactly what Julie was looking for. We didn't find out until after the wedding that the body suit didn't quite cover everything you could see through the dress, but we fixed that with a little Photoshop magic! But finding rings for the ceremony really stumped us.

We wandered the streets peering into shop windows looking for a solution to our ring problem. We were almost at the point where we were going to get the mood rings that change color when you put them on your finger that you find in a souvenir shop, but I was a bit afraid of putting it on Julie's finger during the wedding and have it turn the color of "disappointed" or "furious." Fortunately, we found the solution at the last minute. Just as the stores were getting ready to close, we found this one shop on Rúa do Vilar that sold stainless steel rings. They cost ten euros apiece so we could easily afford two, but Julie said she was fine just using her engagement ring for her wedding band. Again, Julie is very accommodating when it comes to rings!

So, we completed our pre-wedding-day scavenger hunt, and went to check in to our fancy room at the Parador. Considering the royal family still stayed here when visiting Santiago, the term "king-size" bed had a certain significance that I had not before pondered. We woke the next morning with our final errands to run. We picked up the dress, perfectly altered, as promised. I needed a haircut and Julie wanted to get her nails done. We parted ways and headed out into the city. It was raining off and on throughout the day, which was typical for this time of year in this part of Spain, and I was a little concerned that Julie might get lost in the labyrinthine streets of the *casco viejo*.

I found a barber who understood the imperative of a good haircut on one's wedding day, and he rose to the occasion. I expected to be done before Julie, but as the hours passed, I began to get concerned. I decided to get dressed for the wedding while I waited so that Julie could have the room to herself when she got back. When she finally returned, she was a bit, shall we say, flustered. Her nails looked great, but she went on about the trouble she had communicating at first with the ladies at the salon and how long it took them, and how she was getting worried they wouldn't finish on time, and then segued to how she was thinking she should have invited her parents to come, and maybe that was a mistake...and.... *that* is what pre-wedding jitters looked like. I decided to go down to the lobby and let her get ready on her own.

Antonio had arrived and was waiting outside the entrance in the Plaza del Obradoiro. He had invited his girlfriend and her daughter, and his sister and her boyfriend as guests to the wedding. They were all dressed up and very excited about the ceremony. I told him that Julie was upstairs getting ready but that she seemed a bit agitated from the nail salon episode. He assured me that everything was going to be fine and showed me a bouquet of flowers he had bought for Julie to hold. They were perfect. It had stargazer lilies, which were Julie's favorites. How did he know that?

As we chatted there in the plaza for a bit, the clouds began to clear, and almost on cue, the sun came out just as Julie appeared at the entrance to the hotel. She was smiling. Antonio was right, she just needed some time to herself to get ready. Antonio greeted her with a kiss on both cheeks and handed her the bouquet of flowers. Julie was a vision to behold. The dress was perfect, the shawl brought out the natural color of her hair, and her warm brown eyes sparkled above the flowers. A ray of sunshine practically led us to the entrance to the church.

Two red velvet curtains covered the entrance to the chapel of La Corticela, which had been reserved just for this occasion. The chapel was in the back of the cathedral, which was filled with tourists and pilgrims visiting this famous landmark, but the reserved sign in front of the chapel truly made us feel like VIPs, as we walked past them in our wedding attire and could see folks looking on as if something special were about to happen. The priest was there to greet us, and he closed the velvet curtains behind us as we prepared to begin the ceremony.

The entire wedding mass was conducted in Spanish, except for the Gospel reading, which Antonio ironically read in English, despite confessing to not speak the language. As Catholic rites are pretty universal, if you had been to a wedding before, it was easy to follow along even if you didn't speak Spanish. Julie teases me till this day that the whole thing didn't count because she didn't know what she was saying, but she clearly said *"Sí, quiero,"* when prompted by the priest if she wanted to marry me. That, of course, is the equivalent of "I do."

There was one point in the ceremony when my heart stopped, because I didn't know what the priest was saying. He asked for *"las arras"* which was not only a word I didn't know, but also a custom I did not know. Fortunately, Antonio had thought of that too, and without hesitation the priest was handed thirteen shiny new coins. The priest blessed the coins, placed them in my hands and instructed me to give them to Julie while repeating the words he said. Then he instructed Julie to pass them back to me repeating the same words. The words we recited generally translated to "Everything I have is yours." I later learned that the tradition goes back to the middle ages when the groom's family paid the bride's family a dowry, but now the exchange of *"las arras"* just symbolizes that the couple shares everything in their marriage. After passing the coins back and forth, I put them in my pocket and the priest finally gave us the go-ahead to kiss.

I'm not sure who had my camera at the time, as it was being passed around during the ceremony, but whoever did, missed that particular moment. Fortunately, we decided to get some more pictures outside in front of the cathedral, where the light was better anyway. On our way out we saw two German women coming in who we had crossed paths with a number of times on the Camino. The surprise on their faces at seeing the two pilgrims they were used to seeing in hiking boots and backpacks now dressed in a suit and a wedding dress was priceless. Without words they asked if we had just gotten married, and when we nodded in response, they gave us a silent applause and beaming smiles.

After our photo shoot outside in the plaza, the seven of us headed back to the Parador for dinner in the fancy dining room that used to be a wine cellar. We treated ourselves to traditional Galician cuisine, including *percebes*, or barnacles, which I understood are quite the delicacy, and our wedding cake was *Tarta de Santiago*. We were there for hours, and when our waiter saw that all the other restaurant guests had left, he turned up the music and invited us to have a dance in the aisle between the tables.

Antonio then suggested we move the party to a pub called O Galo d'Ouro, (the Golden Rooster in Galician) one of the oldest taverns in the city with an old Wurlitzer juke box, dark wood paneling and cozy tables to share a few rounds of *licor de hierbas* to toast the newlyweds. I don't know if it was the *licor de hierbas* or the mystical muse of the Camino, but a look of inspiration came over Antonio's face and he grabbed a clean bar napkin from the next table and pulled out a pen from his pocket and began writing. He wrote so fluidly, that there was no doubt this was not his first time putting pen to napkin, and no doubt the words were coming from some place he had tapped before. And when the pen stopped moving, it was finished. He looked at it, as if he were reading the words himself for the first time, and then he handed it to Julie and me as a wedding gift to bring the evening celebration to a poetic close. This is what was written on the napkin:

Y Dios dijo sí, en su amor fue Adán
Y Adán dijo sí, en su amor fue Julie...
Y la materia comenzó un baile imposible en el tiempo
Y titilaron las estrellas
Y nacieron los labios en los besos
Y el calor en los abrazos
Y la sal en las mareas.
Y los amantes ataron su sombra a la noche
Y sus ojos a la luz que ciega, al deseo, a la ternura,
        a la palabra que ama, que salva, que crea
Y Adam y Julie fueron palabra, fueron amor,
        fueron camino, fueron mar,
        serán futuro y esperanza, serán ellos siendo dos,
        serán uno, serán amigos.

I hate to translate this, as just the act of doing so would somehow take away some of its magic, the magic it created in that moment. But, so as not to feel I am cheating the reader or leaving them no choice but to resort to Google Translate, where I am certain that no magic lives, I will do my best to capture what my friend wrote that unforgettable evening.

And God said yes, in his love was Adam
And Adam said yes, in his love was Julie...
And matter began an impossible dance in time
And the stars twinkled
And lips were born in kisses
And warmth in embraces
And salt in the tides
And the lovers tied their shadow to the night
And their eyes to the light that blinds, to desire,

> to tenderness, to the word that loves,
> that saves, that creates
> And Adam and Julie were word, were love,
> were journey, were sea,
> they will be future and hope, they being two,
> they will be one, they will be friends.

All that on a bar napkin. No edits. No cross-outs or
erasures. Just a single stream of consciousness from the
heart of a good friend, transcribed through pen on a napkin
that was more accustomed to soaking up whisky than ink.
That was not the last time that Antonio would take pen to
napkin to capture one of life's important moments, but those
are for another story.

Julie and I left O Galo d'Ouro, bid farewell to our friends,
and headed back through the alleys of Santiago to our royal
wedding suite to spend our first night together as husband
and wife. The next morning, we packed up our hiking boots,
grateful to them for carrying us this far but glad to not have
to lace them up and walk even one more kilometer. Our
pilgrimage along the Camino had come to an end and we
swapped our boots for flip-flops, rented a car, and drove
south to Portugal where we would spend our honeymoon on
the warm sands of the Algarve and dip our feet in the healing
waters of the Atlantic.

The Yellow Arrows

"Estáis perdidos," said the driver of the car as he rolled down his window.

It was somewhere along the Camino many years after Julie and I had walked that stretch of road on our way to get married.   I had returned to Spain to join a seven-day pilgrimage organized by the University of Santiago for a group of Brazilians. My plan was to scout out this program to see if it would be appropriate to bring my students the following year so that they could experience being pilgrims along the Camino de Santiago. I had been walking that day with our guide, Juan. He had a degree in geography and was pointing out all kinds of fascinating things: the change in architectural styles of the buildings, what caused the color of the water in the streams we passed, the names of plants that lined the road we were walking, and theories about the sounds that chickens make when communicating to one another. I don't remember what exactly we were talking about at that moment, but we were so caught up in conversation during our walk that we were quite startled by the car that had pulled up next to us to tell us that we were lost.

The driver pointed in the direction we had come to say we had missed a yellow arrow about two kilometers back. We thanked the man before he drove off, and turned around to retrace our steps. We couldn't believe we had walked so far without realizing we were no longer on the Camino. We laughed at ourselves, recognizing the irony that in our roles as guide and scout, we had gotten lost and didn't even know it. As we headed back up the road, we agreed to talk a bit less and stay focused on finding that yellow arrow.

I have often thought how nice it would be if everywhere in life there were little yellow arrows telling us which way was the right path to follow, and if there were Good Samaritans who would point you back in the right direction should you veer off course.

As I think back to that year I got married and Julie and I walked the Camino, I believe there were many yellow arrows pointing me in the right direction, and not just the ones painted on the road to Santiago. I think of that first summer I met Julie and wondered if she was the one, and then there were all those odd coincidences: the song on the radio "Hey Julie" sung by a guy from New Jersey named Adam, and that romantic movie we stumbled across about a person from Boston and a person from Philadelphia falling in love, and that episode of Law and Order talking about a character named Adam and his girlfriend Julie, and the banner with the words "Jules Rules!" that we passed by on our first date in New York, or that the name of the bar where our relationship first started was London, the same name of the city where Julie's relationship with her first husband ended.

Were all of these odd coincidences some kind of karmic yellow arrows pointing me in the right direction, telling me Julie was the one? And what about the Good Samaritans along the way, like my cousin Joanna, my friend Antonio, the old Spaniard from chapter one, or the four nurses? Is there some supernatural power giving us clues along our journey in life and sending us emissaries to help us stay on course? Our first Christmas together, a mere week before we got engaged, Julie wrote this in a card she gave me:

"If anybody had told me last Christmas that I would be spending this Christmas with someone I was in love with, I never would have believed them. I didn't think that I was ever going to feel the way I do about you. I know that we discuss (and joke) about religion often. But you do know that I believe in God, and I truly believe that He brought me you. The best Christmas present I could have ever wished or hoped for."

When I think back on how I had just gone to confession that Easter telling God that I was ready to find love, and then, a couple of days later, out of the blue, I get the e-mail from my cousin asking if I would meet her friend Julie, it is hard not to believe God had something to do with it.

I know, many of you are now thinking that I am just being a Pollyanna, and it is not so easy when you suffer through really difficult times, and you look for the yellow arrows but just don't find any. And what about those who don't believe in God? Are there still mystical yellow arrows out there to be seen to help us on our way? I know that this story of mine has been, for the most part, one of joy and love, but don't think that I haven't also experienced those moments of doubt and despair. There are times when things can get so dark, that it is hard to believe that God even exists.

I am reminded of an episode of the television show The West Wing, when the President, played by Martin Sheen, is talking with his parish priest, played by Karl Malden. He is trying to make a really difficult decision, and is frustrated that he can't figure out what to do.

The priest asks him, "Did you pray?"

He responds, "I did, Tom. I know it's hard to believe but I prayed for wisdom."

"And none came." the priest replies as if to finish his sentence.

"It never has...and I'm a little pissed off about that. I'm not kidding," says the President.

The priest leans in and says, "You know, you remind me of the man that lived by the river. He heard a radio report that the river was going to rush up and flood the town, and that all the residents should evacuate their homes. But the man said, 'I'm religious. I pray. God loves me. God will save me.' The waters rose up.

A guy in a rowboat came along, and he shouted, 'Hey, hey you in there...the town is flooding! Let me take you to safety.' But the man shouted back 'I'm religious. I pray. God loves me. God will save me.'

A helicopter was hovering overhead, and a guy with a megaphone shouted, 'Hey you down there...the town is flooding! Let me drop this ladder and I'll take you to safety!' But the man shouted back that he was religious, that he prayed, that God loved him and that God would take him to safety.

Well...the man drowned. And standing at the gates of Saint Peter, he demanded an audience with God. 'Lord,' he said, 'I'm a religious man. I pray. I thought you loved me. Why did this happen?'

God said, 'I sent you a radio report, a helicopter and a guy in a rowboat...what the hell are you doing here?'"

(Sorkin, 2000)

It's funny... I just realized this is the second show I referenced that starred Martin Sheen. That was completely unintentional, but I must confess that *The West Wing* is one of my all-time favorite TV series. I would vote for Jed Bartlett for president. Anyway, I guess my point is that just because we may not see the yellow arrows in our life, it doesn't mean they aren't there. And even when you are walking the Camino de Santiago where the yellow arrows are actually painted along the road, you can still miss them.

But if we can find yellow arrows marking our way anywhere in life, why bother making a pilgrimage in some other part of the world? What is the value of leaving our homes, leaving our possessions behind, packing only the essentials, and walking with others whose language we may not know, whose cultures may be foreign to us, whose pace of life may conflict with our own and give up control of our familiar routines?

In simplest terms, it is to discover ourselves. Edward Hall explains that what gives humans their identity no matter where they are born, is their culture, the total communication framework: words, actions, postures, gestures, tones of voice, facial expressions, the way we handle time, space and materials, and the way we work, play, make love, and defend ourselves. And because we learn our culture as we grow up and often share our cultural norms with those around us, we lose sight of what makes us who we are. "These behavior patterns, these habitual responses, these ways of interacting gradually sink below the surface of the mind and, like the admiral of a submerged submarine fleet, control from the depths." (Hall, p.42)

Over time, we forget these behaviors were all learned and just assume them to be innate, and go through life just assuming the way we act is "normal." It is not until we interact with others who do not share the same cultural rules that we find ourselves uncomfortable or lost. And it is this discomfort, this feeling of being lost, that allows us to transcend our own culture and learn not only about the culture of others, but better understand our own.

Those who have traveled abroad or have grown up in multicultural families probably know what this discomfort feels like...but also know what transcendence feels like when you can competently interact in two different cultures. What makes the Camino de Santiago so uniquely transcendental is that so many people from so many different countries and cultures come to walk this pilgrimage road, so that the opportunities for learning and growth are endless. And while you may come away understanding more about others, their languages and cultures, you will most certainly understand more about yourself...but expect to get lost a few times along the way...even if the road is marked with yellow arrows.

Does everyone who walks the Camino return with a feeling of transcendence? Do they find God or some kind of spiritual awakening along this pilgrimage road? I don't know. I have seen pilgrims singing as they enter the city, and crying as they place their hand on the statue of the saint at the entrance to the cathedral, but I do not know their stories. You have now heard mine.

I will forever remember that summer that I chose to walk the Road to Santiago. I found myself. I found Julie. I found love. If my story should inspire you to take a month and go walking through the towns and countryside of northern Spain, then wonderful. But more than the sights, tastes and sounds of the Camino are the encounters with others along the road that make the experience what it is. As Pope Francis explains, "True joy is born from the encounter, from the relationships with others. We must create a culture of encounter, a culture of friendship, a culture in which we find brothers and sisters...They all have something in common with us: they are images of God." I believe these images of God can be found in all corners of the world, and I encourage you to go out and walk with them wherever you may find yourself with your boots on, your walking stick in hand, and searching for yellow arrows. And wherever your journey may take you, I wish you a *"¡Buen Camino!"*

Afterword

It has been more than fifteen years since Julie and I walked the Camino de Santiago together. We are still married. We have two wonderful kids, neither of which have the names we discussed while walking that summer to get married. I am still in touch with Antonio, the best man at our wedding and guide on our pilgrimage. We now have a collection of napkins with poems that he wrote for other milestones in our lives. Both of my parents have since passed away and they never said anything about not being invited to the wedding.

Twice, I have taken a group of students from my school to Spain to walk a leg of the Camino to learn about the language, the culture and the life of a modern-day pilgrim. Many of them have said it was a life-changing experience. The airlines did finally lose my walking stick on my third trip to Santiago, so I now walk with a pair of trekking poles. I have to admit; they are much lighter and easier to pack when traveling, but none of the romance of my Irish bordón.

When my son turned thirteen, he and I walked from Santiago to Muxía, a part of the Camino I had never walked before. He said it was the best part of his summer. I hope to walk a part of the Camino with my daughter when she gets older, too. Someday, maybe when I'm retired and the kids are all grown up, I hope Julie and I walk the Camino again together. We might need to arrange a "sag wagon" to carry our packs if we do the whole thing! I love to look at the wedding album we made on Shutterfly and think back to where my journey with Julie began. I still find yellow arrows in some of the most unexpected places.

References

Chopra, Deepak. *The Spontaneous Fulfillment of Desire*. Harmony Books, 2003

Dickson, Del. *The People's Government*. Cambridge University Press, 2014.

Hall, Edward T. *Beyond Culture*. Anchor Books, 1989.

Jeong, Beop and Ryu, Shiva. *May All Beings Be Happy: The Selected Dharma Sayings of Beop Jeong*. The Good Life a division of Wisdom House Publishing, 2006.

King Jr., Martin Luther. *Strength to Love*. Fortress Press, 2010.

Lewis, C.S. *The Complete C.S. Lewis Signature Classics*. Harper Collins Publishers, 2002.

Merton, Thomas. *No Man is an Island*. Harcourt Brace & Company, 1983.

O'Collins, Gerald. *Catholicism: A Very Short Introduction*. Oxford University Press, 2017.

Regan, Brian. "Standing Up – Lost Baggage." Comedy Central. Clip: Season 1, Episode 1, June 9, 2007. http://www.cc.com/video-clips/vcd88g/lost-baggage.

Rohr, Richard. *The Naked Now: Learning to see as the Mystics See*. The Crossroad Publishing Company, 2009.

Sánches, Mónica, editor. *El Camino de Santiago a Pie*. Ediciones El País, S.A./Grupo Santillana, 2002.

Sorkin, A. (Writer), and Schlamme, T. (Director). (2000, February 19). Take This Sabbath Day [Season 1, Episode 14]. *The West Wing*. Warner Bros. Entertainment, Inc.

The New American Bible. Catholic Bible Press, Thomas Nelson Publishers, 1987.

The Way. Directed, produced and written by Emilio Estevez, performances by Martin Sheen, Deborah Kara Unger, James Nesbitt, and Yorick van Wageningen. Elixir Films, 2010.

Waldman, Peter and Pope, Hugh. "'Crusade' Reference Reinforces Fears War on Terrorism Is Against Muslims." *The Wall Street Journal*. September 21, 2001.